THE JOY OF BEING AWAKE

THE JOY OF BEING AWAKE

Hector Abad

translated from the Spanish by Nathan Budoff

Lumen Editions
a division of Brookline Books

ISBN 1-57129-020-6 (pbk.)

Library of Congress Cataloging-in-Publication Data:
Abad Gómez, Héctor.
    [Asuntos de un hidalgo disoluto. English.]
    The joy of being awake / Hector Abad ; translated from the
Spanish by Nathan Budoff.
        204 p.   cm.
    ISBN 1-57129-020-6 (pbk.)
     I. Budoff, Nathan, 1962-   . II. Title.
PQ8180.1.B33A97   1996
863--dc20   96-31632
                               CIP

Published by:
Lumen Editions
Brookline Books
P.O. Box 1047
Cambridge, Massachusetts 02238

Contents

Prologue

In Which Nouns and Pronouns are Declared.

THAT WHICH SAYS YES, THAT MOUTH IS MINE (A FOUL-MOUTHED character), your humble servant, Gaspar Medina according to other signs, he who writes this, he who dictates these presumptuous memories, the son of my mother... No: idiotic mask. Me. Me me me me me. The truth is in this vexing monosyllable, namesake of all of us, pronoun of which any may believe himself the owner, gadget for the king, the bourgeois, the vassal, the saint, the assassin, magic sound of mine: me. *Yo, io, moi, ich.* Me.

Me, immodest word, me, the name I give myself at all times, me. I am going to remember the mes that I have been from when I began to be me. From when I remember me (a little), from that yesterday's me, plural, distant and varied, right up to today's me who begins to dictate and who now is another, and including that of the tomorrow in which I fin-ish these memoirs of the other me who I will be. A halluci-natory and grotesque hall of mirrors that always repeats the image differently from the real me.

I am here seated in front of the desk, almost immobile, with my mouth that opens and shuts like that of a foolish fish but which doesn't emit bubbles but words, immediately copied down by my amanuensis and read who knows when by you. We are three: my secretary, you, and I. I am named as is written; my secretary is named Cunegunda Bonaventura; you can call yourself by your name. The three of us and this paper. Without lies or false modesty. Since I am the one who is dictating, since I am the judge, since I am the eccentric demiurge, you should know now that I am the one who gives the orders around here. Only me. A clumsy God, for the moment, with a secretary as his ventriloquist. And not as his ventricle, not yet. Is it clear? Me, she, you, and this paper. Like in the first grammar classes, Iam youare heis sheis theyare. One who speaks, me; one who writes, she; one who reads, you, thanks to our companion, this paper. I want to seem methodical, orderly, because I know that later I won't be. I am not capable. Or I don't feel like it. I jump from here to there. My memories are a pack of echoes that bounce around my cranium, voices that both bark and bite.

Of the two dates, the crib and the grave, the beginning and end of each of us, I am very close to the latter and extremely distant from the former. But I am anticipating too much for a prologue, the vestibule of a book where we greet one an-other. There will be time and pages to say everything. Every-thing: my sayings, nonsense, dictates and taunts: everything.

Reader (if you exist), I know that I am not worthy of having you enter my house, but one word of yours will be enough to energize me. Reader, I know that you are not worthy of setting foot in my house, but one word of yours will be enough to create me. Reader, I know that I am not worthy of having you enter my house, but one word of yours is enough to heal me.

You will see the people I have known, the cities in which I live, the books that I continue to read, that which I thought and think, the little that I did and the even less that they did to me. Stretches of experience and pieces of me which might finally coincide with me. Fragments of that which I lived, not in the order in which they proceeded, but instead in the order in which they withdraw from oblivion. This is my index, not the finger, but the summary of my life. And this is my index, this time the finger, which rises up and returns to me to rest on my sternum while one more time I say: me. Me. Me period. That which I have come to be, if I am something, after all that I have been.

One

In Which the Kiss of Eva,

the First Woman, is Spoken Of.

I REALIZED THAT I WAS WEALTHY WHEN I WAS ABOUT FIFTEEN, during the same period when I discovered that kisses are not shared only with the lips. I think that my innocence was largely due to modesty, for until adolescence I knew that we were *comfortable*, a word that for me meant easy chairs or a garden... anything, but not wealth. I owe both revelations to the tongue of the same person, Eva Serrano, the daughter of some friends of my parents.

Eva was one year older than me and, like me, an only child. Her family was Chilean, but they had been living in Colombia for a few years. On the weekends, when they came to visit us in the country, while the adults submerged themselves in interminable games of canasta, Eva and I had the horses saddled up and we went riding on the trails that passed near the country house. Sometimes we filled the saddlebags with provisions and stopped to eat out along the trail, by the edge of a waterfall. I didn't know then that in literature loves are consummated on the banks of babbling brooks, but it was there, among the murmur of the cascade, that Eva revealed to me the mysteries of my economic situation and the passion with which it was possible to give a kiss.

That sudden entrance of a tongue in the forbidden space of my mouth continues to be one of the greatest surprises of my life. It had never passed through my mind that in addition to forks and toothbrushes, any other strange body could invade the frontier of my lips, much less that blunt, humid muscle. Many years later, in the basilica of the saint, in Padua, I realized that everyone else had always understood the importance of this permanent guest of the mouth, as was evidenced by the worship as a venerable relic of the incorrupt tongue of Saint Anthony. Sucking a pacifier, savoring a fruit, distinguishing sweet from bitter and from salty, articulating sounds, these were the only functions that my tongue knew until Eva Serrano appeared and opened my mouth and my understanding to other possibilities.

Many times I have asked where she, at such a young age, could have learned to kiss that way, but now it doesn't matter to me. That she was very conscious of my family's economic situation, on the other hand, quickly became clear to me. Her father was employed by a multinational corporation and the salary he earned, though good, had never permitted them to possess certain things which my family treated as natural privileges. The bite of this disparity, together with the constant financial insecurity of the Serrano family, had made Eva permanently aware of our easy chairs and gardens, that were, clearly, the wealth of my house. This mixture of money and tongue led me at times to think (but it's an occurrence which I now reject, for it stains the memory of my first woman) that the linguistic kisses of Eva were a strategy devised by her mother to try to consolidate an advantageous engagement. In any case, I was lucky enough that my first experience caught me off guard in both of these matters, in cash and lingua, two elements that—like no others—influence the beginning and end of matrimony. Since in my house speaking of money was forbidden, I didn't know, until Eva told me, that I was a good catch.

My loss of innocence didn't consist, then, in the union of our respective and chaste genitals, a process which my father had already explained to me with the aid of several illustrations of the Encyclopedia Britannica, but in the union of tongues. Of this humid contact neither my father nor the Encyclopedia Britannica spoke. I remember well that upon our return from the country house I went straight to our library to consult the article appearing under *kiss*, and afterwards with growing alarm, the section *tongue*, without discovering the answer I was searching for. Even now I recall those tomes of my father's, full of theory but lacking practical information, in which a kiss is the act of pressing or touching with the lips, the cheek, the hand or lips of another, as an expression of love, affection, reverence or greeting. The hand, the cheek, at most the lips of the other, but not the tongue. Then the article spoke of the *osculum pacis*, but this didn't interest me either. I naïvely thought that the solution could be in the article *tongue* and the result was disastrous, for although it provided mountains of information (that the tongue was a mobile muscle found in the majority of vertebrates, that it was located in the lower part of the mouth, that it was very useful for speaking, masticating and swallowing), it didn't include a single word about kissing. It even maintained that the tongue can inform us about bits of food that get stuck between our teeth, but about kisses not a word. It appeared that Eva's tongue was much wiser, that it knew more than the Britannica. Thanks to her I became acquainted with the humid carnality of two open mouths in contact. And from her tongue I also received the revelation of what comfortable really meant. But I am repeating myself.

After my failure with the encyclopedia, still in search of enlightenment and consolation for my ignorance, I revealed the affair to my Uncle Jacinto, brother of my mother, an old sick monsignor, during my obligatory weekly visit to my relatives. My uncle listened in silence to the story of the kisses. Without saying a word he rose from the armchair which served as his confessional and with his ravaged fingers pulled out one of the volumes of his extensive library. With great solemnity he asked me to listen. The book he had chosen was a book of Saint Jerome, it was written in Latin and Uncle Jacinto translated a piece of the text which went something like this:

"By the order of Emperor Valerian, in the year 257 of our Lord, a martyr in the flower of his youth was taken to a pleasant garden. There, among white irises and red roses, while by his side twisted a crystalline brook with a sweet murmur of water, and while the wind caressed the treetops with a calm rumor, the martyr was stretched out over a bed of feathers and left there, deliciously bound with braided garlands so that by no manner could he escape.

"When all the others left him, a beautiful harlot appeared. She grasped the martyr's neck in a voluptuous embrace and—this is disgraceful even to relate—began to insistently caress his sex; after having excited the libidinous appetite of the body of the young man, the shameless conqueror endeavored to lie with him.

"The soldier of Christ didn't know what to do or what path to take: the cruelest torments hadn't defeated him and now voluptuosity was dominating him! Finally, responding to a celestial illumination, he bit the tongue with his teeth until he cut it off, and he spat it in the face of the woman who was kissing him: thus the intensity of the pain replaced sensuality and he was able to defeat her."

I must confess that on that afternoon in my memory (and even today) I didn't know if the martyr had bitten his own tongue or the harlot's, but either way I didn't dare follow the advice of Saint Jerome and my uncle the monsignor. I continued kissing Eva by the edge of the waterfall, although each time that we exercised our *pange lingua* and her *corporis mysterium* erupted impetuously into my mouth, it almost made me laugh to think of the risk that was being run by this meaty appendage of that fair maiden.

To tell the truth, if the apathy of my character hadn't begun to manifest itself even then, I wouldn't have had any problem in formalizing my engagement and being married to Eva. Even today, on those rare occasions when I am incapable of understanding the insanities which men commit chasing after some lips, I close my eyes and I recover in my memory the flesh of Eva Serrano; it is only in this distant and neat interval of memory that I am able to understand the lustful deliriums of men. I must recognize that I unfairly judge the mother of Eva Serrano by insinuating that she was the interested procuress of our adolescent flings; she would have been, instead, like Celestine, one who was able even to excite a cold stone, and she almost succeeded. Eva Serrano is the owner of one of the few human bodies which I still remember with a certain appetite. When all is said and done, now that I read again, with surprise, books that I have already read; now that I encounter friends on the street and fail to recognize them; now that I travel to well-known places and arrive at unfamiliar locations; now that I begin an Our Father and end in a Hail Mary; now that memory is a tangle of confused echoes, if I close my eyes and I leave my lips slightly parted, I can yet feel her tonguey way of kissing.

Two

Which Narrates a Contrite Confession of Perfect Chastity and Colorless Indifference.

CHASTITY, FOR ME, HAS NEVER REQUIRED ORDERS OR COMmandments. In high school, during the confession, I remember the skeptical and malicious smile of the chaplain before my repeated negative replies to his inquiries about purity. His interrogations were so detailed that they obliged me to think of something completely foreign to my experience. My astonished face did not satisfy him and my naïveté did not manage to convince him, so I had to invent sins against the sixth commandment just to leave him relaxed and to prevent him from constantly warning me, before absolution, that the sacrament of penitence lacked validity if the spoken confession was deliberately incomplete. Mine came to be so complete that it exceeded the limits of thought, word, act and omission. After having had to lie about subtle caresses, glances never exchanged and temptations that didn't cross my mind, I was obliged to confess to having lied, so that he would pardon me for the sin of having confessed sins of imaginary lechery.

This tranquility of the senses seems to be something that comes to people of my age, but I arrived here without ever straying out into the world of desire, or maybe I started here. In my youth the idea of being a psychological eunuch haunted me, but I must explain that my lack of appetite has nothing to do, as far as I know, with profound frustrations or with barriers erected by an overly rigid morality. In reality I would like to have suffered, like everyone else, that fount of tortures and delights which the realm of the voluptuous must be.

Don't think that I didn't search for objects with even the slightest hint of generating lust. There isn't a perversion which I haven't tried to practice. But in vain, for masturbation, zoophilia (swans, hens, sheep, donkeys, horses, dogs and even salamanders), homosexuality, gerontophilia, pedophilia, sadism, masochism and virtually anything you can imagine, never troubled my peaceful spirit. Now it has been quite a long time since I withdrew from my attempts to be like the majority of my brethren. In an inversion of Pascal's equation, postulated several centuries ago, my efforts to be a beast converted me into an angel. Neither the dull predictable commerce of the flowering groin, nor the conscientious aberrations of the divine Marquis, were able to sway the immobile pillars of my indifference.

Before the total absence of lubricious and wanton days, I eventually developed schematic rituals in pursuit of carnality. The anxieties of an intemperate life compelled me to practice for years an extremely methodical and boring masturbation: every Thursday at five in the afternoon. And I'm not counting, as impudent, the unspeakable acrobatics which I had to go through to fulfill my weekly assignment. But I have lacked consistency even in my vices, and many Thursdays I forgot my obligatory weekly manipulation. In the same way I was never able to persevere with tobacco or alcohol or even nervous tics.... Fidelity to my nature obliges me to permanent change.

Nor do I have any physical defect which would serve as an alibi for the precarious activities of my senses. I do awaken, although ever more rarely, with morning erections like any other man; in my youth I donated liters of sperm to the sperm banks, and they never complained of a lack of activity in my donations; my hormonal equilibrium is impeccable, I haven't suffered diabetes, and despite my age, my prostate is intact. At most I could tell you of a premature change of life, which coincided with the date of my genesis.

At times I was tormented (although the verb is undoubtedly exaggerated) by this idea of being a sort of innate ascetic. During my childhood, my parents suffered noting what careless doctors diagnosed as an unusual case of precocious anorexia. Eating has always been a kind of chore for me, an obligatory engagement with your body which one must fulfill. I never was able to recall what I ate the preceding day, and it's still necessary that in the morning, at midday, and at sundown, someone remind me that yet again it is time to eat. On the rare occasions when I have not had a cook in the house, eating wouldn't even cross my mind, and I had to set alarm clocks to indicate to me when the hour had arrived to go to a restaurant and consume lunch or dinner. The word *hunger* is an abstraction to me, no more tangible than the notion of asymptotic lines: notions born in the minds of men, possibly real, but not sharing the indubitable certainty of pain.

Yes, for I possess a much clearer perception of pain. Maybe I owe this to my total rejection of anesthesia, and my incomprehension of analgesics. Our human condition is so precarious, at times so difficult to distinguish from that of plants, that I keep pain as a treasure, almost the only proof that I am alive. I never feared the insertion of needles, nor the blood that springs forth after one of the barber's clumsy movements. On the contrary, these rare moments are mementos of my existence. Thus I was never scandalized by that accessory of the ascetic that was so stigmatized by the followers of the enlightenment, that is the hair shirt. Ah, the bristles and thorns that squeeze your thighs, languid maiden! It's only thanks to those memories that you know you are flesh and not cold stone. Those who haven't been granted the mystic experience of sprinkling an inflamed wound with a generous shower of vinegar and lemon juice know little of life. As far as the other mortifications of the flesh, like fasting, sleeplessness, and vows of silence, they never had any merit whatsoever in my eyes, since they already form part of my natural disposition. Without discussing how modern times have degraded these habits to an inconceivable vulgarity: diets to lose weight have cheapened the sacred fast into a daily regimen, television has made the whole family silent as it shares its complete spiritual withdrawal before this multicolored altar of idiocies; those who pass from discotheque to discotheque pass the whole night awake—drunk on ethereal noises.

In any case, being insomniac, lacking hunger, and being taciturn are qualities of my natural disposition and they have not required monastic rules to develop fully. In the summer when I retire to the ancient vicar's house in Pulignano, in Tuscany, where I have my refuge for my hours of greatest misanthropy, I feel a certain satisfaction on proving that without intending to, I repeat the rhythm and the conventional style of the Cistercian monks. By four in the morning I am waking up and I meditate walking through a hundred-year old olive grove sprinkled with the broken crosses of a cemetery which decades ago stopped allowing burials. A slice of bread and a bit of water are my only morning repast. Then I read, or I begin to... But I'm not going to speak of that now. Of my life in Pulignano, of those more celestial than monastic days that I have passed there, I will speak later.

I also do not appreciate the esoteric delights of drunkenness. I have had, like everyone, my drunken friends. For example, I remember Sergio Valderrama, who spilt chalices of rum (in reality they were glasses) into his esophagus as one would fill a bottomless pit, or at least one that was very deep. I recall his silence turned loquacious due to the imbibed spirits, his timidity shredded and converted into a risky audacity. I, on the other hand, feel drunkenness as a vapid dizziness installed in a clouded mind. Alcohol has a soporific shine for me. If I was interested in sleeping more than the four hours that I now sleep, I would have a few more drinks, but in wakefulness I am less bored than when I sleep.

In gambling, during a few months of my distant youth, I believed I had found, at last, an asylum, a temple of escape. An occasion to dissipate my fortune, to challenge my ines-

capable lucky star. But what a mistake. In the casinos I came
to curse the heavens for my good fortune. What fun is it to
win, win, always win, or at least almost always? So I feel
robbed of pleasure, by an excess of pleasure.

Ah, if I were capable, how I could be a sensualist. Instead
a lukewarm broth or light tea with milk are the most remarkable dishes that my palate and my tongue recognize. But don't
think that my education doesn't allow me to eulogize the
exquisite offerings that are presented to me upon other's tables.
The truth is that I denigrate or eulogize all foods equally. I do
not encounter more delight in swallowing a lobster than a
bowl of lentils (or vice versa, for the defenders of the rustic
cuisine). The preference of men for certain exotic dishes I
understand for what it is, an intellectual weakness, and I
believe that most people, if they think about it seriously,
would agree that chicken would be just as exquisite as par-
tridge if one were able to invert the available quantity of
each of these two aviators. I swallow with discipline, without
feeling that I am performing a penitence or chewing on glory,
kidney, caviar, Mexican tortillas, gringo hamburgers,
Andalucian gazpacho or bread and water. I don't see the difference between a beef loin with peppers, a fried blood sau-
sage, or a boiled cauliflower. For if I don't know what it is
that I like, I also don't understand the finickiness of those
who refuse to eat frog's legs, a plate of brains au gratin,
Santander ants, or bits of rancid camel marinated by the
desert sun. My stupefaction is the same before cookbooks
and metaphysical treatises. What they analyze doesn't matter
to me at all: I don't care about them, and maybe I just don't
understand.

That the world could be magical, or that it is enchanted, as some of my friends who are filled with pious invisible illusions maintain, is an invention of other people and for other people who are not like me. Stripped of superstitions I lean out the window and although I admit that the landscape isn't bad, it is hard for me to discover the dazzling marvel, the perennial enthusiasm, the secret relationships, the impalpable energy. Nothing. False signs, signs only of themselves, apparent messages that don't want to say anything. I do not believe in miracles, nor can I see in the chain of accidents that capriciously combine men and things, a secret design of providence or a predestined event of history. I disembowel the rules or the tricks from all improbable magic (or if not, I know that someone will), and I remain with the distasteful flavor of he who is on guard for tricks. I, priest of nothing, don't rest on the cane of mystery. And what I don't know I face without horror, firm in my bastion of incertitude. I don't give resonant names or obscure explanations to that which I don't understand: I suspend my judgment and I repeat, "I don't know, I don't know," without any great collapse in my self-esteem. If I hear noises on the roof, I think first of thieves, rats or wind, without wasting my imagination on ghosts. Only the foolish have answers (foolish ones) for everything; even before the hateful but definitive nothingness of death, they bring out their exasperating hope of some impossible beyond.

Life, an alien adventure; the earth, a common and senseless grave where Hitler and Saint Francis, my father and his assassins lie buried; love, an imaginary exercise; the body, the source of all evils.

This last paragraph I dictated for the benefit of the confused, but it's not true, or really it only tells half-truths. For life can be, beyond doubt, one's own adventure, and the earth the stage for adventures like love, that parenthesis from exasperating reality, and the body can be both the source of all delights and the source of the most absolute indifference. It is the source of all—the body—of death as well as of love. And this is the wonder of generalizations, viewed from where they are coming from, they are categorical truths that are completely useless.

Three

*In Which the Memoirist Declares
How Well He Was Educated &
How Bad He Tried to Be.*

THERE IS NO DOUBT THAT I RECEIVED WHAT COULD BE CALLED
a meticulous education. I have even thought that maybe
my passive temperament is due to this lack of errors in my
upbringing. My deceased parents were refined people who
had, from the little that a son comes to know, a harmonious
marriage. During my childhood and early youth, a private
tutor and a nun offered me the first rudimentary cultural
lessons. He was secular and liberal, while lacking any sparks
of rebellion, and she was, obviously, Catholic, but never sanc-
timonious. I don't remember ever being severely punished by
my parents. Discounting my lack of appetite, which preoccupied them a little, they said that I was a serious and industri-
ous boy. I was always supremely gentle and, by temperament,
prone to compromise. Without being lazy or self indulgent, I
was always patient and tolerant with others. From very early

on I accepted as one of my maxims the Christian advice of suffering with patience the imperfections of my fellow man.

In high school, without ever being first in my class, I was always closer to the brilliant student than to the careless. I did well on exams although I never copied. And not because I wanted to be honest, but because even then I knew that what one manages to copy, in general, are someone else's errors. If I had a problem during my school days, it was a persistent suspicion of hypocrisy. The nun who accompanied me explained that at times virtue can awake envy. It is much more comfortable to cast into doubt your own virtue's authenticity, than to approach another's excellence. But I never tried to disprove the suspicions of my companions. On the contrary, with the intention of assuring them of the exactitude of the image which they had of me, I engaged in mischief which neither attracted me nor interested me. I made trouble for the sole purpose of not offending others through my good behavior. Also , I have to admit it, because it annoyed me some that they called me "Mr. Perfect." That lack of critique in my nickname, that shadow of doubt, the insinuated suspicion of deep-down pretense, was my only problem in school.

Certainly at times teachers and students took advantage of my good-natured condition and my obliging spirit. They abused my helpful disposition and secretly pulled my leg when they felt they could get some advantage from me. But I never wanted to acknowledge these jokes, as I felt it was cruel to deprive them of the pleasure they took in my naïveté. In any case, even though there is a great insistence on virtue, if you insist (even if it's without great effort) on being generous and accommodating, if you don't raise your voice to answer, and if you are disposed to turn as many cheeks as are necessary, in the end you create more resistance than admiration. The image of virtue is at times more hateful than that of infamy. It was thus that in school I had to embitter the pill of my good behavior and confess, as I have already mentioned, to sins which I had not committed, or perform misdeeds which were repugnant to me. But then again, "repugnant" is a bit exaggerated—I could more realistically say that evil has always left me indifferent. It doesn't attract me; I don't require it; I have never needed to rob or damage anyone, nor desired my neighbor's wife.

I hardly retain any memory of my bad actions. Evils committed without bad intention leave very little remorse. Nonetheless, unmotivated evil doesn't lack a certain diabolical *je ne sais quoi*. I remember that our Spanish teacher had problems with spelling. While we were writing compositions in class, I would raise my hand and ask about the spelling of words whose spelling I knew perfectly well, simply to get the teacher in a jam: "Excuse me, Professor, How do you spell *erudition?*" And he would fall into the trap of the "s" or "t". If I asked about *thoracic*, there was always a blunder with the "c" or "s", or with the spurious "o" of the word *spurious*. But I didn't take pleasure in his innocent slips, I swear, and I didn't share in the happiness of the few classmates who were aware of my feigned inquisitions. I wasn't interested in taking advantage of the prestige I could win among my colleagues; I only wanted to, clumsily, make my tongue happy. I say *clumsily* because at that time I had not yet thought of nor written one of my first aphorisms: "Incorrect spelling is writing's bad

breath." And what satisfaction can we gain by asking someone with a smelly mouth to exhale into our nose? Since then
I have tried to be less brilliant and more intelligent.

Another cruelty, vile in this case, consisted of arousing
the religion teacher. His homosexuality was a secret widely
spoken of throughout the school. At the end of class, after
two hours dedicated to denouncing the loss of values, the
decay of honest ethics, there was a certain charm in approaching his desk and, as if by mistake, brushing his side with my
pubis. That blushing of his cheeks, that flapping of his hands,
that irresistible twitching of his thighs were the evident signs
of his excitation. The model student who, all innocence,
with the face of an angel, asked him questions about moral
decadence, was also the vehicle of his perdition. The religion
teacher's sleepless nights were filled with these insoluble di-
lemmas. But neither in these cases did the complicit laughter
of the majority of my classmates, who noticed the trickery,
delight me. Of this premeditated tormenting I conserve a
memory similar to remorse.

I was also an accomplice to malevolent and gratuitous
tricks. Like searching with some companions in the lunchboxes
of the simpler students, unfolding the plantain leaves which
held their *tamales*, opening one side of the corn paste, spitting into the bacon and capers, returning everything to its
proper place and watching afterwards, full of hilarity, during
lunch, the unconscious delight with which the victims chewed
their balls spiced with a sauce of foreign saliva. Cloaked in
virile generosity, but really with a perversity taken to more
sophisticated extremes, someone would inform the object of
the trick, once he had finished eating, of the presence of the

wrapped-up and gulped-down phlegm.

This exalted school where I received my primary education was largely a temple of charlatans. And I was a fine
example, as I have already explained, proving myself adequate
by inventing sins never committed and performing pranks
never desired. Well, to tell the truth, I committed and re-
lapsed into a sin that I never believed to be one. And that
was to read any of the books that I encountered in the library
of my house. There I discovered the pleasure that the as-
signed readings from school never gave me, which if I remember correctly were limited to censured editions of *Lazarillo*,
more mutilated even than Lazarillo himself; *The Maria* without kisses or praise of the blacks, and a few chapters of *El
Carnero* that I can't imagine how they were able to purify.
The classics, one had to read the classics, but these, for them,
were at most a few of Calderón's soporific *Autos sacramentales*.

In this affair of readings I remember that I had the support of my father, who at times called me into his presence
and, with a solemn pontifical gesture of enlightened origin
that encompassed the whole library in his arms, told me:
"Read what you want, for the books that aren't appropriate
for your age, you simply will not understand, they will bore
you, and you will go on to others until you encounter your
own."

I remember, with horror, one of those sins of a dangerous
document. Thanks to my paternal blessing I flaunted my prohibited titles, until a miniature *auto-da-fe* taught me to hide
my preferences. Without understanding even a bit of what
was written in it, but to be contrary, one day I appeared on
the school campus with a book from my father's library: *The*

Gay Science. The chaplain, with an interested smile, asked if he could borrow it. Months passed and he didn't return it, until finally I screwed up my courage and asked for the book. The priest said to me: "There are books that give our minds indigestion. By the sole act of possessing a book of such gluttonous depravity we have fallen into temptation, if not into sin. I will not return it to you. Even if I wanted to I could not, for I have done you a favor. I burned it. In the middle of the patio of the school I made a small bonfire with my own hands, and I burned it." Ah, if the Gaspar Medina of those days had been even more disobedient and had read his father's whole library, he would have been able to answer with one of Quitapesares' phrases: "Those who burn books, sooner or later, end up burning human beings." But the boy that I was remained mute before the news of the bonfire of the head chaplain.

I also remember the expulsion of one of my colleagues. He was called Juan Jacobo Rodo and he was one of the boarding students, as his family lived in the Cauca Valley. All of Juan Jacobo's life, I can now say, would become a chain of persecutions; his rebellion never was reluctant. But of the chain of Juan Jacobo's heroic acts, the dreamer, I will speak in other memoirs, if I have the strength to write a committed novel. Right now I only want to present the first episode of absurd reprisals in his life.

One night Juan Jacobo brought to his room and to his bed a little girlfriend that he had found in the working-class neighborhood which surrounded the school. He was caught red-handed (that is to say, with *him* inside); the disciplinary commission listened to his impossible excuses, and then they expelled him. Juan Jacobo told me, furiously, that several months earlier they had discovered him in the same bed and in a similar position (although a different orifice) with one of his classmates. Both he and I knew that they had caught many other boarding and day students masturbating together in the showers. Nothing had ever happened, except for lukewarm admonitions. When he was informed of the irrevocable decision to expel him, Juan Jacobo protested the inconsistent nature of the punishment in the two cases. The father rector called him aside to tell him: "My man, Rodo, the solution is very simple: young boys don't get pregnant."

Neither he nor I knew that in the schools for the rich, the protection of the patrimony is more important than the protection of chastity; it wasn't a moral question, but a practical one: going to bed so young with an adolescent girl could lead to pregnancy, to truncated studies, to a marriage with a person of lower social rank. I remember how Juan Jacobo and I were offended by an action we considered hypocritical. We thought that certain institutions had been erected with an ethical temper immune to double dealing; we still had not read certain books and we committed the crass error of attacking the Church without understanding, as Quitapesares understood (also too late), that in reality the Church is a potent corporation with which it is very convenient to remain affiliated.

For all that we dress them in sanctity and happiness, high schools full of adolescents are torture chambers (well, not for everybody, not for the torturers). There we prepare ourselves to see the premiere of the most abominable crimes that we will see repeating themselves throughout the rest of our lives. There we come into contact with all the types of people that we will encounter further on in our lives: the flatterer, the thief, the assassin. Only rarely do we also get to bump into the just. My classmates had that privilege.

Four

In Which Conjectures are Made about the Scent of Sanctity & the Secret Dimensions of the Breast are Given.

IF I WERE NOT AFRAID OF SEEMING PRESUMPTUOUS, AND EVEN considering that I am not a believer, I would say that I am a saint. I believe that all confessions, be they of sinners or angels, are designed such that the reader draw this conclusion. I am writing in generalities, and I know that stories hate abstraction. You don't say "Pepe Garcia was greedy;" instead you recount an episode when he fought over pennies at the corner store. That's fine, but movies and television have bored me with these implicit and prolonged narratives. The word retains the rapid virtue of the abstract. I don't explain why I am a saint, I say that I am. I, instead of trying to demonstrate it in five hundred pages of actions, correc-tions, and repentances, declare it without blushing in three words: I'm a saint. In four: I am a saint. And I'm not even concerned if you think I'm presumptuous, for the feigned fears that are inscribed in books are mere rhetorical figures that don't capture anyone's real benevolence.

It is clear that the opinion which the reader is forming of me due to these pages does not matter to me very much, nor does it matter to me whether he be benevolent or malignant in his judgment of the scatterbrain who is dictating them. Vanity, at my age and in my condition, is an anachronistic residue of youth. Neither condemnation nor panegyric, if either should appear, will change one white hair of my hard head. It's certain that there is nobody so old that they can't live another year, but nevertheless what remains of my life cannot be counted in decades. My repugnant illness, of which I will not speak right now (although I'll add that it's not gout) makes it clear that it is through pure obstinacy that I remain attached to life. And in these last hours or months that I still retain I have resolved to put into play that last plaything of old age, that is this untidy memory which dictates to my amanuensis a few experiences quite possibly disfigured by distance and fantasy. To my secretary, yes, to you, Miss Bonaventura, stenographer of my misadventures, custodian of my secrets. I implore that you transcribe without modesty the following:

My secretary is twenty-five years old, much less than half my age. My secretary copies that which I dictate with periods and commas. She types it up when I am tired, and I reread the transcript so that I can add corrections. A few corrections, not because there is so little to correct, but because if I exaggerate, I could lose my life in a single phrase. Miss Bonaventura knows which phrases have given me the most doubt, she knows that I have had to re-draft the scandalous parts dozens of times, but she wouldn't admit it. Everything must seem spontaneous, like this confession.

Where were we? I was maintaining that I am a saint. Yes, if you can define an apathetic temperament that way, one who is not good by choice or effort, but simply because it's natural. More than a man of great qualities, I am a man lacking in defects. This lack is my only attribute.

My uncles who were priests educated me to be a saint, and this is the result. It's not my fault, I always wanted to be, in the worst sense of the word, good. But nothing. At my age I continue to be a saint though I have done almost the impossible to avoid it. For I have been a saint not only without claiming to be one—that's the least of it—but also without wanting to be one. I have never liked my privileged condition. The traditional saints resist temptation. I have tried almost the impossible to find temptation, without encountering it. Oh Lord, make me fall into temptation! But nothing.

After a few compelled pranks during my early youth, I have limited my acts to a point which is in line with total inactivity. I have already said that I am not a lazy person. Waking up early and getting up has never been a torture for me. It's true that thanks to my family's situation I have never needed to work, and if I have worked (very little, why should I deny it), it has been only for my pleasure. I have trustworthy people who are charged with maintaining and even augmenting my patrimony without requiring either my intervention or my presence. I have plenty of money at my disposal and I waste it, save it or share it according to my whims. Those who verify that money has no importance are correct,

as long as one has plenty of it. Only those who don't have
enough cash live preoccupied with it, much as those who
talk most about sex are those who rarely practice it.

In relation to this, between me and my stenographer there
is not even the most hidden of sexual activities; the most
that one could find would be sporadic, brief and almost casual corporal intercourse. Nothing serious: a filial hug, a slap
on the buttocks. I present her, to whom I am dictating, as
witness. And don't think that Bonaventura is an ugly woman.
One of my weaknesses, possibly the most serious, is that I
have never been able to endure the company of ugly people.
Their mere presence makes me uncomfortable, annoys me,
impedes my thoughts, or obliges me to think only about the
arbitrary unhinging of nature which permits such mishaps.
Thus, well, Bonaventura is not an ugly woman. Being my
secretary she couldn't be, or at least I couldn't be dictating to
her.

Even more than this, to please the curious readers, and
those with an attentive libido, I am going to copy down the
detailed description which my friend, Quitapesares, once made
of the body of my amanuensis. There he, the author of the
description, or his ghost, affirmed that the breasts of Ms.
Cunegunda Bonaventura are among the few perfect things in
the universe. Here I have the page written by my Quitapesares:

"Evolution produces breasts like those of Cunegunda
Bonaventura every two or three centuries. There must be a
secret *pi* figure which represents the perfect dimension of
breasts, and this number should be measured once and for all
in the tits of Medina's secretary. Once he permitted me to
touch them, in his library, and my hands were embraced by

them almost completely without fully embracing them. It was like feeling that one completely possessed a breast, but that at the same time this completeness always lacked something, a reserve of desire, to be fully consummated. The degree of turgidity was also incomparable. They weren't like a fifteen-year-old's tits, which can be too firm, or like those of the forty-year-old with silicone implants. If a pillow manufacturer were able to measure the softness of Bonaventura's bosom, it would give him the recipe not only to make insomnia impossible but also to make waking up impossible. On that same occasion I tested the texture of the skin, and my tongue slid across the breast of Cunegunda as if its skin were an ice cream, only warm. The circle of her nipple was briefly disturbed upon contact with my tongue, and its skin, until then a bit smoother than that of the rest of her breast, became completely uniform over the whole breast, except in its color which passed from rose to an intense pink."

Together we finish reading, entertained, my libidinous friend's exaggerated pectoral description. Due to an old weakness as a reader, which obliges me to always try to confirm all of the descriptions which I read, I ask my amanuensis to show me her breast at once, and I reaffirm to the reader that what the lecherous Quitapesares sustains is almost certainly true. And now that I am using the verb *sustain*, my secretary does not require mammary support. If I was a pig, like my friend and like the majority of men, right now I would fear letting my hand draw close to Bonaventura's body. I can do it with complete innocence. Yes, she is here within reach of my arms (more precisely: her left breast is in my right hand), writing down what you are reading, but there is no desire in my fingertips and I can only make aesthetic appreciations. I don't doubt that there are people who get excited before a marble statue of a platonic Venus; but if some do not get erections in front of statues (and not even while touching them), think that this same thing is exactly what happens to me in front of the pectoral perfections of Bonaventura.

She knows, for example, that she can urinate in my presence, and so we have brought a chamber pot into the library. Thus I am not forced to detain the thread of my thoughts due to the simple fact that my secretary has a corporal necessity. Urinating seems to have something in common with yawning: both apparently are contagious. Thus Bonaventura, while I dictated to her the section about her occasional urinations, had to drop her skirt and panties and let the yellow stream of her innocent urine roll down. I have just stood back up after submerging my index finger in the warm liquid of the chamber pot. Now I am sucking on my index finger. I believe that after a few hours of dictating I begin to have a salt deficit. This is the only reason that I do it, believe me. The reader shouldn't imagine that he will encounter here wild pages of sex, when there are good writers who write them, and even better ones who don't.

Look, Borges also didn't speak of his bed, and those seeing-eye dogs he shared it with. I don't claim to be comparable to him, I don't aspire to acquiring the perfect frigidity of his writing. I see well and I don't suffer from trembling; I don't write with my own hand because of custom, and because it seems more comfortable to unravel the tangle of my thoughts without being preoccupied by calligraphy or the constant missteps of my fingers over the keyboard. Quitapesares says that writing is speaking without being interrupted. Well, that's exactly what dictating is. My dear secretary, let me thank you once again for your good works, and permit me to deposit a perfectly paternal kiss upon the still-wet root of your thighs.

I said that I was a saint. An exaggeration. Seventy-two years of living can make us a bit self-indulgent. But I don't know why I revealed my age. The long speeches of the old will be of little interest to the young (and the majority of men seem young before me). It would be better for me to say that I'm a twenty-seven-year-old youth who imagines himself with the numbers of his age inverted. But in that case all this that I am writing would be a falsification, and I also doubt that people are interested in lies. Finally. In any case, what least interests the reader are digressions. So let's return to where we were: I am a saint. Or almost.

This I can say, since I know myself and I am dictating. Suspect the omniscient, the omnipresent, the demiurge who in the third person can say whatever he wants about me and spread it to the four winds. As my truth is mine and only I know it, I present my acts to demonstrate it. I distrust the supposedly impartial and believe, although not always, in this tremendous me, my only owner. Let the malicious say what they will, only I know that I am a saint. A saint, although maybe I am exaggerating.

Five

The Highly Improbable Explanation
for Gaspar's Refuge in Turin.

I WAS BORN IN THAT REGION WHICH RESIDENTS OF THE FIRST World like to call (with paternalistic disdain) the Third World, and I plan to die in that region which residents of the Third World like to call (with filial reverence) Europe. In reality I have passed at least half of my life in this privileged part of the earth, although always with one foot here and the other there, with my eyes gazing at one place while standing in the other. A foreigner in both worlds (and without being a nobleman), when I travel to America I don't know if I am coming or returning, and when I fly to Europe I don't know if I am leaving or arriving. But it would be better to proceed in an orderly fashion.

To explain the circumstances of my voyage to Turin, my First World city, I have to go back in time and recall Medellín, my Third World city. The explanation for my trip to Italy, if I think about it seriously, is rooted in several automobile excursions in my childhood. It was during the first years of the decade of the thirties, and there weren't very many cars in the city. But my uncle, my mother's brother, was the Archbishop of the city, and the gringos of United Fruit had given him a luxury vehicle, just like those used by a few high officials from Washington. The story of this car, of its ignominious ending, as well as of the blindness and recuperation of my uncles vision, I will recount further on. Now I must explain my remote relationship with Italy, explain how I came to be in this country, why I have pretended to work here, and why I am finishing my days in this Turin which populates my imagination as fully as that other rhyming city which bleeds profusely in South America.

The uncle—and his chauffeur-driven automobile—came to pick me up once a month. He didn't enter the house, but he had his driver get out and come fetch me while he waited wedged into the back seat, rosary in his hand, enclosed in the twilight formed by the closed curtains of his black Chrysler. I entered through one of the hulk's rear doors, and I felt my face burning as I kissed his ring. My uncle tried to be pleasant and he patted me on the knees. His cassock was impeccable and the purple color of his socks matched exactly with the waist band and the round hat on his head (my mother explained: it's called a *solideo*, meaning 'only to God'). My uncle was uncommonly large, slow like an ox, and he inspired in me the same irrational fear that large gentle animals instill in me. The unctuous chauffeur called him "your excellence" in his local accent: "Shall we leave, your esselence?"

"Shall we pass by the palace first, your esselence?" We toured parishes and vicarages throughout the archdiocese or we went to call on some bishop from the region, to whom a visit was due. We left early because, wherever we might be, at midday, mass was celebrated in the church. During the ceremony I sat on one of the front benches, and demonstrated all of the fervor and devotion that I had learned from my nun. I knew all of the prayers by heart, I am sure, although today even with the Credo, I am unable to get beyond "all that is seen and unseen."

In the back seat of the car one almost never spoke. I would drift in and out of sleep on the thick, embroidered leather cushions, and I wouldn't wake up except when my uncle drew back the curtains for a moment to see where we were, pulled his solid gold watch from his pocket (the same one which I now extract from my pocket to inform Cunegunda that it's almost twelve), gazed at the time and sighed due to our delay. During the whole journey he would continue sifting his slow rosary between his thumb and index finger. Occasionally, suddenly, he would call out names of saints and I and the driver were obliged to answer, if it was towards the beginning of our travels, "*llevadnos con bien*" (move us in safety), and if it was towards the end of our tour, "*ora pro nobis.*" These saints' names didn't arrive arbitrarily in his mind; reality, for my Uncle, consisted of a network of associations around patrons of the church. Thus, if there was a car accident, he said "Saint Christopher;" if we passed a bookstore, he said "Saint Geronimo" or "Saint John of the Cross;" if a black man crossed the road, he said "Saint Martin;" if the oafish chauffeur ran over a dog, my Uncle would commend it to Saint Bernard.

The Archbishop was in the habit of showing me the projects undertaken due to his initiative: "There we are building a seminary;" "In that building we will locate the school of engineering;" "Behind those pine groves we have some land and we are going to build a retreat center for laymen."

Afterwards I would fall back asleep, but my drowsiness was always disturbed by the unexpected name of some saint pronounced in a strong voice and without any warning. I remember one time we were returning from a nearby town, and as we passed a housing project called Saint Barbara my Uncle mentioned the name of the location. The chauffeur responded, like a shot, "*ora pro nobis*" and my Uncle reacted with a quick "Idiot," muttered under his breath.

My Uncle spoke with a French-style "r". This fascinating and unusual pronunciation, together with its origin, are connected to my travels to Italy. My uncle said that he had picked up the habit in the Piedmont, in Turin, where he had studied in the seminary with no less than Giovanni Bosco, later canonized a saint. While he spoke of his years of study he had the habit of caressing my head and he told me that someday he would send me to study with the Salesians in Turin. Turin was never the goal of any tourists or travelers, and was even less frequented by South Americans. Except for Erasmus and Nietzsche, who finished going crazy there and ruminated on kissing horses, few people choose this Italian destination. Thus I am sure that when I had to choose a city in the world in which to find refuge from the violent ignominy of my land, I picked Turin out of fidelity to the memory of my Uncle, by then dead for quite a few years.

It's true that, based on my Uncle's memories, I also could have elected Rome as the goal for my Italian life. I have the impression that my choice was influenced by the fact that my Uncle's memory of Rome seemed mundane, and even in a certain sense repugnant to me. On the one hand there were the audiences with the Pope, which he described in a courtly tone, with the ritual of kissing the ring finger, and the genu-flections and memorized phrases in ecclesiastical Latin. And on the other hand there was something that the Archbishop never told me about but which I learned of in the agonies of his dying outcries.

The delirium had to do with a singer whose acquain-tance he had made at the dawn of the century in the capital of Christianity, and it referred to his voice and the unusual effervescence of his songs. It was curious, but my Uncle mixed a Donizetti opera, *Lucia di Lamermoor*, with sacred psalmody from the Sistine Chapel. "Ah, your voice, your voice, the velvet of your irreplaceable voice!" There was something embarrassing in his gasping outcry. So much so that my other Uncle, Monsignor Jacinto, felt obliged to explain, to extri-cate us from the trap of our evil thoughts. Nothing like what I (or my hypocritical and *frère* reader) began to imagine, no, none of that. It turned out that in Italy my Uncle had be-come an aficionado of *bel canto*, with a very discerning musi-cal sensibility. We had never known of this passion in Medellín, and it was only his brother who could reveal to us that year after year, in absolute solitude, the Archbishop lis-tened ecstatically to an antique recording of a Roman singer.

The future Archbishop had, there, in 1901, made the acquaintance of the last Master Singer of the Sistine Chapel, maybe the last *castrato* in the history of music. This eunuch sang the sacred psalms by day; and, during opera season, he sang arias in the theater by night. My Uncle, shortly before he was ordained, had seen him dressed as a woman, sing the role of Donizetti's Lucia de Lamermoor. And he had confessed to his brother that he would never again hear a similar voice, unless the times re-valorized ancestral wisdom.

I have said that in my country he never acknowledged having enjoyed, or still enjoying, that mundane vice of opera, too frivolous and improper for such a high officer of the church. At any rate it was no sacrifice for him not to hear them since, as Uncle Jacinto revealed to us, in private he confessed that the voice of the *castrato* was the only one which gave song its celestial dimension. Ever since some modern prelate had eliminated that sensible rule that only men could sing in the Sistine Chapel, the magnificent profession of *castrato* had disappeared. The moral conscience of an unhinged century (which cared more about sex than music) had deprived man of the voice of the angels. But he had the strange privilege of knowing and hearing the live voice of the last adult child anointed for song. Since then and forever, music would never be the same.

I don't want to be unmasked as a lying saint. The "r" of a priest who had studied with Giovanni Bosco: Could that really be what brought me to Italy? It's absurd and it's not true. Neither was it the sun, the adventures, or the hot light which the Nordics pine for—for if one thing is abundant in the tropics it's the sun, as well as heat and adventure. An imperial past, ruins, the pagan language (mother language of my tongue) converted into a property of the church, Christo-

pher Columbus. Wine, castles, olives, ties, canals, bell towers, seas with famous names, islands. No, none of that. Nor
would a hypocritical memory of a castrated singer impede me
from arriving in Rome. No way.

The truth is that I arrived in Italy by coincidence. I stuck
my index finger on a map of Europe (with my eyes closed)
and the tip rested on Turin. The story of the bishop was
merely posterior rationalization. Upon seeing Turin underneath my fingerprint, I thought: What do I know about that
city which will determine the shape of my future? I had only
one reference, the distant memory of my Uncle's seminary,
the monthly rides in his luxury car during the same years
when they canonized Giovanni Bosco. That was all I knew.
Upon electing my First World city I didn't even know that
the imposing Italian automobile factory of Turin was located
there, nor that there was a great publishing house where the
love of my life was working, nor that there was a famous
museum full of mummies. I arrived on the site of my prob-
able tomb the same way that newborns arrive in the place
where they are born: without prejudices.

Six

Which Deals with Two Clerical Illnesses, Banana Growers, & an American Automobile.

SUBMERGED IN THIS EXERCISE WHICH EXPOSES A CERTAIN TRIVIAL nostalgic weakness, I had almost forgotten the other promised stories. Humming an aria from "The Marriage of Figaro," *Voi che sapete*, my uncle's favorite, I began to fall asleep in my library's easy chair, when I felt the warm breath of my secretary close by my left ear. She wanted to remind me that the account lacked the story of the car and the gringos. I warn you that the story is long and less edifying than my story, but at the same time since they are unrelated happenings, it is saved from being too boring. Additionally, at this point in my absent-minded biography, there shouldn't be only one lonely protagonist; everyone has the right to have their stories told. I will add them so that my dear secretary Bonaventura doesn't fall asleep, like me, nor continue whispering words into my ear. She likes the concrete, but also loves symbols and she wants to know about the blindness, at once both real and emblematic, of my uncle the archbishop.

My uncle was the bishop of Santa Marta during the days when, within his diocese, a memorable massacre was committed. So many laborers were assassinated in the slaughter that writers of pregnant imagination (many years later or many years earlier) have been able to fill interminable wagons with the dead. The story of the massacre of the banana workers, curiously, has always been written by the losers. Everything is told in detail in novels and history books, but I'm not going to deal with the public details. I will tell the private history of the Bishop, which my mother revealed to me many years ago at an evening get-together. Behind the President who ordered the Minister of Government, who passed the message to his colleague in the War Department, who gave it to the Governor of the Province, who transmitted it to the Military Commandant, who translated it to the official, who gave the order to fire to the murderers, there was, as always, a group of gringo banana growers. Not that they were going to get their hands dirty; I'm sure that at the sight of the blood of the decapitated chicken they were eating for lunch they would have fainted. But a word dropped at the club, another in the ministry, and another while leaving the church, works miracles in the tropics (bah, also in the temperate zone). And this the bishop, who wasn't an obtuse person, knew.

I insist that I am describing reality and not inventing emblems. It's not my fault if at times reality entertains itself by imitating the schematic fantasies of allegories. The day of the killings my uncle lost his sight. I mean he became blind, literally. I wouldn't play the trivial word game of making him go blind only because he pretended not to see. No, it's true: my uncle, that very day, went blind. You don't need to tell me that he didn't go mute also, I know that, and I'm not excusing him. Let me tell the story: the same day as the killing of the banana workers my uncle turned blind, and three months later the gringos who hatched the massacre sent him to Rochester to receive, free of charge, an operation that allowed him to recover his vision. When he returned, few traces of the killing remained. The humidity and the torrential rains had swept the blood into the sea, and the only thing that remained in the ambiance was a memory faded by fear and an echo of quiet rifles.

My uncle, at the petition of the national government, issued a public declaration which diminished and almost completely negated the responsibility of the authorities and the troops in the killing. He, a cerebral man from the interior, had never completely understood the hot temperament of the coastal people and once had even come to write that "the sunny lands of the coast are refractories of the sun of divine grace." In the document about the strike which he dispatched at the request of the government, my uncle sustained that "excluding a few complaints presented by the parish of Aracataca, and a few moral mistakes committed by one or two officials of said location, he was unaware of criminal acts on the part of officials, nor had he heard that during the strike the troops had robbed or burned, raped women, violated or murdered women or children." As you can see, at least my uncle had the prudence not to give any testimony regarding the assassination of men.

The black car of my memory had come along on the ship
returning from the United States. And as if it were just a
little thing, a very few years later (which is a lightning bolt of
time for the church) an unexpected letter arrived from Rome:
the ascent to Archbishop and the consequent transfer to a
more important city of the interior, the same city of his ancestors, where he was born, Medellín. Thus the killing could
be forgotten, at least for a few years, until a reoccurrence of
blindness returned to remind him of those memorable times,
albeit of unfortunate memory.

It is difficult to accept the less heroic aspects of my family: I would rather summarize them. Our lineage has a tradition, I must acknowledge, of indifference to the motherland,
of eyes fixed on other places, more towards the north or east
than towards the land where we were born. My uncle the
archbishop's great-great-great grandfather (and that of my
mother, to be exact), was a high-commissioner of his peninsular majesty. After the calamitous independence (to which
the Medinas were always opposed), all of the oldest sons down
to my grandfather preserved the tradition of being named
honorary consuls of the Motherland. My uncle would not
have become a bishop without the recommendations of a
Spanish cardinal who had maintained relations with the family,
and I myself would not have committed the greatest error of
my life if it weren't for the letter of another cardinal, but
that's another story. In any case I fear that all of this feeling
ourselves *hidalgos* culminated with the generation of my uncle
the archbishop, if I exclude myself.

As to the details. The first refers to the car that United
Fruit gave him. This change of point of view or of cultural

reference, the movement from Europe to the United States, precipitated the ruin, if not in financial terms (for certain members of my family conserve their fortunes), at least in terms of pride and prestige. I am not going to speak of the swell of my relatives, lost in the north, missing in the meandering curves of capable North American dullness. They all studied there: Colorado, Minnesota, Kansas... and they returned with that insufferable attitude of rapid and efficient executives, of bankers without prejudices, of specialists in the wrinkles around the eyes, converted into Yankees with chewing gum, silly jokes, rhythmic music, cocaine, tennis shoes, Walkmans, jogging and many other horrors. Youngsters without nobility, which is exactly what *snob* once meant, *sine nobilitate*.

The disaster was announced by this North American gift, my uncle's Chrysler, which ended its journey crashed and burned. I write *Chrysler* to be realistic; really it could have been a Packard or a Ford or a Buick. Even today, in the declining years of my existence, I am unable to distinguish between a Mercedes and a Volkswagen. I know that my uncle's was a large black automobile, it was American, the rest doesn't matter to me.

What matters to me is that the Archbishop's sneaky chauffeur liked to take whores out in the Ford or in the Packard, or in whatever it was, in that big black car of my gray memory. At night he would secretly sneak the car out of the palace and on that same seat, which by day heard only the whisper of the rosaries of his eminence, at night the most abject carnal crimes were consummated and boasts of the lowest appetites were heard. The fervent prayers of the day converted into the impudent curses of the night. The sighs of Christian commiseration converted into the moans and groans of miserable selfish pleasures. The gossips began to talk, and finally the scabrous affair, which for months had been whispered about in the houses of all the best families of my city, arrived at the ears of the most interested party, the Archbishop. It was the final rage of his life and the first time that I heard him swear: "I'm the last to find out, like a cuckold!" And he tore the tablecloth from the table upon which he was eating, breaking the plates of fine French porcelain, hurling the fine silver, making the Murano pitchers fly in fragments, and an inhuman scream ran through the long corridors and the innumerable rooms of the palace. After excommunicating and firing the chauffeur, almost at blows, after lighting the car on fire in the first patio of the palace, my uncle went to his office to draft his letter of renunciation. "If so many things occur before my eyes without my being aware of them, it means I am not capable of properly fulfilling my functions."

The odd thing was that after burning the car and signing the letter he began to feel the same symptoms of that first instance when he lost his sight. A few months later, now completely blind, when the dispensation arrived from the Vatican, he walked through the long corridors of the palace for the last time, and then he went to live in the house of one of his sisters, my old maid aunt, Marujita.

The last memory that I have of him is in her house, sitting at the head of the table, completely blind, poking his plate with a fork, trying to hook a piece of potato. To his right my aunt Marujita, and to his left his other brother, Jacinto—also a priest, but only a Monsignor, and parish priest of Aracataca during those same days of the killing.

It's true, time and suffering had done their damage, but it would be too easy to say that this trio was the perfect image of decadence. Silent and grand, much taller than the average citizens of Medellín, with their well-kept hair a pure white, hers up in a bun and the men tonsured with a perfect circle on the crown of their heads, with the table set as in the best of times, you could tell yourself that they didn't lack dignity even amongst other signs of disaster.

It was all captured in the image of Aunt Marujita, who suffered from Parkinson's disease. When the servants passed with trays of food, she insisted on serving herself, even though in the trajectory from the tray to the plate she would lose half of the servings. Watching her eat was a torment, for each mouthful represented an enterprise. When she was eating soup, she held her spoon just like the rest of us, but she had to draw her bowl much closer to her face so as not to spill the broth all over herself. The forks of rice never arrived full at her mouth, and the dog always sat at her feet because with her droppings, he ended the meal as full as his owners. Although she saw perfectly well, it was just as difficult for her as it was for the Archbishop to locate a bit of meat on the plate, and even more difficult for her to carry it to her mouth. Luckily the servant served the rolls with butter already spread upon them, and only filled the glasses of water up halfway, for the glasses too overflowed in their passage from the table to the head. The old Monsignor, nasty with his old jokes, said that his sister was capable of making a mess eating a banana.

But the worst of the three, if I can say it, was precisely

him, Monsignor Jacinto, even though his vision was good and he didn't have Parkinson's. Unlike his brother, who wore new ones with an Italian cut, he used old cassocks, shiny from many ironings and dusted with cigarette ashes. During meals he tied a large napkin, big as a sheet which reached all the way down to his knees, around his neck. He gulped down his soup using a silver spoon, but he didn't hold it with his index, middle finger and thumb like the rest of us; he grabbed it with his fist, like the peasants. It's not that he had less refined manners than his brother and sister. He held it this way because he had practically no fingers.

In the times of the banana growers, being the parish priest of Aracataca, he was unable to deny the evident brutality of the army and found himself obliged to speak more openly about the incident. He had even published a tract explaining his version of the events, which, even if it was carefully enunciated with measured and relatively diplomatic words, was very different from the official version. This scrupulous accounting of the patient historian made the evidence of the disorderliness and the massacre obvious. The Papal Nuncio and the Cardinal—after receiving a sign from the Minister of War, who had just had lunch with the American ambassador—had no room for doubts, and they had confined him as Chaplain in Agua de Dios, a well-known leper colony. The permanent contact with the sick, along with the tremendous hygienic deficiencies of the colony, had been the cause of infection.

His hands scared me, but I always fell into the hypnosis of staring at them. I stared and stared at them without daring to ask anything. The five fingers seemed to only reach to the first joint, resembling five fat toes stuck to his hand; the fingernails didn't start at the end but in the middle, almost as if they were extensions of the phalanges. They were thick fingernails, cylindrical and twisted, like an old dog's. When he finished his soup, he lit a cigarette, holding it prisoner with excessive force between any two of his stumps of fingers. He smoked without respite, and without caring about the ashes that fell onto the white napkin, the linen tablecloth, onto the porcelain plates saved from the fury in the palace, and finally over the glossy and ash-covered cassock. He smoked until he burned the butts of his fingers and his round fingernails, until his brother, with a sharpened sense of smell due to his blindness, upon sensing the singed flesh would advise him: "Jacinto, careful, you're burning yourself again." My uncle would then put out the cigarette butt, take off the napkin, and without regard for the carbonized bit of his stump, he would drink down in one gulp a whole glass of water, picking it up with both hands (as if it were a chalice), and then he would go ahead and light another cigarette.

After dessert they adjourned to the private chapel of the house. Aunt Maruja, Uncle Jacinto and the dethroned Archbishop got out their beads and we all began to recite the rosary. The servant girls sat a bit behind us. There were four of them in all, three more or less young ones and an old woman, Tata, who had worked with my great-grandparents even before my uncles were born. She had started as a maid when she was seven years old, and now she was nearly ninety. She was completely deaf, and blind in one eye; with her good eye she saw stains and shapes, and she prayed the rosary following her own rhythm, for while she was at the "now and in that time," we were repeating in chorus "blessed art thou among women." But nobody reacted—except me, at times I couldn't control my laughter; I have never been able to accustom myself to irregularities, not even when they are repeated every day.

A moment of inactivity free of guilt: that is the rosary. At least that's what it is for women, and especially for the women who are servants in my country. At no other moment of the day can they be quiet, inactive, one hand upon the other, without being accused of laziness. Finally a moment in which you don't do anything, you rest, you recite a relaxing melody and think about whatever you want to. And the best things about the rosary were, at the end, the litanies to the Holy Virgin. I don't know a combination of sounds made by the human voice with a greater sedative power. There is no agitation which they can't tame, no intranquility which they can't dissipate. They are an opiate, a dream, an innocuous drug that the wicked modernist Council tore from our mouths.

Even now in these final days of my existence, if I occasionally become anxious and suffer from an impatient insomnia, I begin to recite from memory this monotonous and harmonious singsong that contains the only phrases that I know (without understanding all of them) in our true Mother Language: *Sancta Maria, ora pro nobis, Santa Dei genitrix, ora pro nobis, Sancta Virgo virginum, ora pro nobis, Mater purissima, ora pro nobis, Mater castissima, ora pro nobis, Mater inviolata, ora pro nobis, Mater intemerata, ora pro nobis, Mater amabilis, ora pro nobis, Mater admirabilis, ora pro nobis, Virgo prudentissima, ora pro nobis, Virgo veneranda, ora pro nobis, Virgo praedicanda, ora pro nobis, Virgo potens, ora pro nobis, Virgo fidelis, ora pro nobis, Speculum humilitatis, ora pro nobis, Speculum justitiae, ora pro nobis, Sedes sapientiae, ora pro nobis, Causa nostrae laetitiae, ora pro nobis, Vas spirituale, ora pro nobis, Vas honorable, ora pro nobis, Rosa Mystica, ora pro nobis, Turris Davidica, ora pro nobis, Turris eburnea, ora pro nobis, Domus aurea, ora pro nobis, Stella matutina, ora pro nobis, Salus infirmorum, ora pro nobis, Refugium peccatorum, ora pro nobis, Consalatrix afflictorum, ora pro nobis.*

Once the rosary was finished Uncle Jacinto would call Snowflake, the dog whose color is obvious, whom he would lift up onto his knees to scratch with his thick-fingernailed blunt digits. At the end of these demonstrations of affection Uncle Jacinto's shiny cassock was covered with white hairs that Aunt Maruja, through the chaotic movement of her hand, tried in vain to remove using a fabric brush. After the effusions with the dog my two priest uncles retired to the library, he who was able to read would read, while the other would meditate. There were various framed letters there, on paper bearing the seal of the Vatican, and signed by the Vicar of Christ. Written in Latin, they said, for example, that *Jacintum* was declared a monsignor and that he could give as many masses as he wanted to in the chapel of his own *domicilium*.

Uncle Jacinto, when he wasn't praying, eating or caressing the dog, read. He was an untiring reader, and on the title page of each book he noted in his calligraphy made illegible by his maimed hands, the date and time when he began to read the book, and on the last page the date and time when he finished, along with some brief comments. He didn't have that reverential respect for books so common among both the illiterate and bibliophiles, that is to say among those who don't have books or who have them only as adornments. While he read, Uncle Jacinto grasped a pen in his fist and often stopped to underline something with a not very firm and stable stroke, or to scribble along the margin some erudite reference. He didn't restrain this habit even when reading old manuscripts, and the proof of this is an edition I have of the Confessions of Saint Augustine, published in Italy in the Sixteenth Century, marked with his twisted underlining and his distorted commentaries.

Years before, at the beginning of his illness and when in the rainy seat of the Nuncio they exempted him from service in the leper colony, his brother had entrusted a nearby parish to him, and he still went there to celebrate mass. He consecrated and delivered the sermons, but he didn't give communion. In the beginning he had been obstinate in his insistence on giving it, wielding theological arguments: if the host was, literally, the body of Christ and nothing more than the body of Christ, it couldn't be contaminated by Hansen's bacillus, nor consequently be contagious. But the parishioners understood little about scholastic subtleties, and they would only receive communion from the other priest. Thus Uncle Jacinto stood there waiting, with the unpolluted paten and the goblet full of hosts, for some parishioner to stick out his tongue; serene and steadfast, my mother said, but with a broken heart.

It was in those days that, to complete the already excessive measures of his guilt, Uncle Jacinto had an impious thought which he would later attribute to a suggestion of the Enemy. Why, he had asked without measuring carefully the deeper consequences of such a question, why had our Lord only occasionally cured lepers? Why in his infinite power had he not cured all lepers once and for all? Why, if it was in his power, not eradicate Lazarus' disease from the world with one unique, magnificent, definitive blessing?

In those days when we made our weekly visit to the uncles, I didn't have the slightest idea of what had happened to Uncle Jacinto's hands. I only knew that, along with the blindness of the retired archbishop, it was the punishment and the greatest test that God had imposed on our devoted family. They were convinced that true life was earned with the sufferings endured in this one; a conviction which carries sacrifice to masochism. I hope that there is another life for them, for this one they wasted in permanent suffering.

You could say that since the days of my uncles and even since a much earlier time, the human invention which has exercised the greatest fascination over my family has been the invention of God. I myself have become enraptured caressing the dimensions of the largest creature to which man's imagination has given birth. The force of God is such that he has acquired a reality as great as or even greater than the major characters of literature. Even Quixote has university departments, institutes, houses, libraries and magazines, but not a single temple.

Ah, God, that human fiction, benevolent for most, and merciless for my two uncles. The worst part is that both the blind man and the leper died convinced that the punishment which Our Lord had sent to them was well deserved, one for not having seen the massacre and the other for having tried to defend the victims. This conviction—being the logical

result of a belief immune to contradictions—was wholly impervious to the fact that they couldn't conceive of atone-
ments so severe for such opposite behaviors.

Seven

On How the Attempt to Make a Self-Portrait Can Result in a Grotesque Masquerade.

POTENCY AND BEARING, THOSE TWO ATTRIBUTES WHICH SO preoccupy men, have been of little importance to me. I touch Cunegunda, and that reaction of the eunuch capable of living in the Gynaeceum with neither nightmares nor evil thoughts, doesn't cause me any anguish. When I look in the mirror I observe without pity or preoccupation the irresistible signs of old age. I have a vague memory, sustained through the power of photographs, of my image at fifteen, at twenty and at thirty years of age. Since then everything has been a continuous descent, with brief recuperations and sudden relapses. In the morning, without a shirt, I brush my teeth and I contemplate, without feeling sorry for myself, the amorphous, weak, gelatinous ripple of my chest. I attain nothing by contracting my pectoral muscles, for this undulating mass is no longer controlled by any fiber. But I am so pleased with myself, with my clean teeth (still my originals) that I smile at the mirror. I don't make even the most minimal concession to those distant pangs of conscience advising me to do a bit more exercise. This doesn't bother me, just as the wrinkles on the forehead and the profound blue circles under the eyes of a sick man don't bother me. Sure, although they don't bother me I am aware that this negation of bother demonstrates an act of deliberate conviction. It is not a positive attitude, it is not that "I like them," but rather the attempt to neutralize a verb which assaults me.

Will I sketch my portrait? I can only say that now I don't feel anything for this body defeated by the years. Once I had a different, better skin, but it's not possible for me to become attached to all that. Let me say something about my character. I would say that I detest (the verb is exaggerated, but I understand) seriousness. For me, life has never been a weight. Pornography and hagiography entertain me (or bore me) equally; neither does the first excite me, nor the second exalt me, but my life doesn't pass like a Sunday in front of the television. I don't flee boredom in dull, inane activities. That's what I say, and I say it even though the preceding phrase sounds a bit serious to me. I am contradictory, yes, just as I have two feet and two hands, two eyes (the analogy is not mine), each one with its own manias. Bah. I'm old and I'll die soon. I live my last days in this parenthesis of being between two nothings. Death, or life, are like certain books and certain movies: one is not afraid of their ending, one simply just doesn't want them to end. You don't fear everything which you don't desire. But this isn't a definition, or it doesn't claim to be one. It's only saying the following in a long-winded way: I am not afraid of dying; the truth is I just don't want to die. But why do I use so many words to say something so simple? I simply disdain that desert which is approaching. To die is to fall into nothingness, in the total nothing, and thus it has no relationship with me, since I live and think.

There will be those who will opine that my apathy keeps me from realizing an intense life. No. This distance permits me to not waste time in stupidities. That's it. Attending clients, making telephone calls, revising the bank statement, paying bills: the life of the others. Cry because the thieves broke in, for the wrecked car, because they dyed my hair badly, because my daughter got a C in school, because I can't find the check: the life of the others. I will seem arrogant, I will seem to be a fake noble, I will seem to be an unbearable *hidalgo*; they will speak of my ivory tower and they will be right, but I won't live the life of the others nor will I give a damn about my nobility, my supposed elitism, my house of ivory or anything else which everyone attributes to me. Opinions are also part of the life of the others.

It's ridiculous that in an autobiography one isn't capable of sketching one's self-portrait. But I have Quitapesares, my friend, who has written my description or profile, what would be read at my funeral if I die tomorrow, what he knows or thinks he knows of me. He says: "Gaspar has a neutral face, perfectly inexpressive. He doesn't have a serious or severe face, I would say more serene. Exalted, absorbed, he seems to live in another place, and think about other things which he doesn't communicate to anybody. Think? One often wonders if Gaspar has any thoughts, any questions, anything which perturbs him. Rarely does he listen when you speak to him, and although he tries to look at whoever speaks to him, his gaze gets lost, it drifts off into nothing. He seems to always be looking inside. He doesn't look his age. There are few wrinkles on that face which has never made a grimace, or any emphatic gesture. Vacant, like in ecstasy, fascinated by something he doesn't disclose, he seems as if he were always just passing through or just visiting. He undervalues everything, including himself. He speaks little, with dry and sure phrases that nonetheless don't express any certainty, and that seem to get caught halfway. Those who know him immediately hate him or praise him. A few are finally able to like him, but he offers very little in return, and may not even be aware of them."

Just like you would ask a painter friend to paint your portrait or a photographer you might know to portray you, we should do the same with writing. Ask our friends to describe us in words. I ask Bonaventura to construct my spoken portrait. I order her to write whatever occurs to her, and she obeys with this:

"Don Gaspar Medina is my lord and my boss. He doesn't know that he has beautiful hands; he doesn't know that when he rests his hand on one of my breasts I dissolve inside. Don Gaspar believes he is cold as ice and old as Methuselah's father. Maybe he is. But, like the ice, he melts, and he fascinates like Methuselah. Don Gaspar now says that I shouldn't write with the stale metaphors of dead poets. He is a tough judge, but as the previous writer said, he's also tough on himself. He is more indulgent with me. If he were less harsh on himself, he would also feel that something happens to him when he touches my breast. He has white, white, brilliant hair, the same color as the beard which he sometimes doesn't shave. When he shaves it makes me angry. I want him to let his gray-haired beard grow; it would hide the ironic grimace of his mouth, the cynical smile. Sometimes I don't understand him, I don't know if he is scolding me or teasing me. I think it's both things at the same time. Now he is looking at me and I don't know if he likes what I am writing about him or if he'll tear it up. I smile at him, but he doesn't smile back at me. Quiet as a sphinx. I write this word and he asks me (I don't know if he's scolding me or teasing me) if I didn't mean to write *effigy* instead of *sphinx*; he tells me that sphinxes have tits like me and not fallen and spongy chests like his. I say that I meant to say quiet as a statue with excavated eyes and a vacant gaze. It's very difficult to like Don Gaspar, it's true that he doesn't let you. Now he has infuriated me and I won't write anything else, period. Why does he make fun of me? I add only that he doesn't always have the gaze of a statue; sometimes he has the gaze of a painting, alive, and from wherever I sit, it seems like he was looking at me."

Will this book be my effigy? Yes, the effigy of forgetfulness. Making a portrait of yourself, even if it's your passport photo, is an exercise in vanity. When the photos come out we anxiously look at them to see if the result matches our self-image. I am looking at my hands, old skin divided into five plus five cracked fingers with dry fingernails. Bonaventura writes merciful lies. Upon dictating "merciful lies" she has left, indignant. I have to finish my exercise in ink alone.

I pick up Cunegunda's pen with my stained hand. I want to insist, in my own hand and letter, that the body hasn't mattered to me. I make a decision: I take off my clothes and begin to write on the skin of my legs with the pen. At times hairs get in the way (although now they aren't very many), and it will be difficult for Cunegunda to decipher these alphabetical signs. I use my convex stomach as a folio, and like blue veins my writing covers this hide thrown out of tune by time. What word shall I write on my member? Over my heart, on my chest I write that from time to time a few women were able to wind it up. On my fallen left arm I write a lame hendecasyllabic litany:

I have my own skin upon which to write,
one hand rhymes with the other hand,
verses that don't merit the time,
when not read by eyes that are kind,
read by a tongue licking and wounding my mind,
whose waters are made of neither fire nor lime,
licking until it reaches my elbow or some other land,
of this, my body, which is as poor as it is grand.

Bah, these verses are a stupidity and I'm not able to write any straighter ones on my back (my hand doesn't reach), and this naked body of mine, where I could reach, is now furrowed with awkward letters that don't describe me, or hide me, that don't denounce me or report me. So much writing on oneself, for nothing. So much searching in writing, to find out that all I say about myself doesn't end up being at all like what I really am.

Well, better than writing is letting others write. What still matters to me are the books I read, where I do encounter myself. This nonsense that I dictate (except for now, since my grouchy amanuensis became infuriated) interests me less and being mine at times seems to have less or nothing to do with me. I have been interested in examining deceptive memory, at times with a joy in deceit, and trying to comprehend time, which sometimes seems sudden as a lightning bolt or slow as one of my girlfriends (whom I will now tell you about). I, like that fondly remembered *hidalgo*, dedicate the moments when I am idle (which are the greater part of the year) to reading books about chivalrous undertakings or about any other things, with such pleasure and enthusiasm that I have forgotten almost completely the usual activities of my class and even the administration of my ranch; and my curiosity and foolishness in this has become such that I have exchanged loves, lands, voyages, and all other types of diversions, just to have a few books to read and time to read them. I have discovered, reading, the joy of being awake.

Eight

A Dictation which Lamentably Sinks into Nostalgia and Pretensions of Nobility.

I SEE MYSELF AT TWENTY-SEVEN, CLOSED OFF IN MY LIBRARY IN the Medellín house. I have turned off the lights so as not to be distracted by my eyes while I listen to a passage of Mahler's Fifth Symphony. After listening to the record for the second time, I turn off the machine. From the darkness I start to think of another place besides my library, my city, my country. I imagine myself living in another place, in Mahler's Vienna, for example, or in one of those cities of the Italian Savoy, which for Flaubert were the most boring in the world. It doesn't matter if I think of myself in another city, among other reasons because the exercise of imagining myself in any other place is too difficult. That me that I was has not been a distracted tourist on the vast continents. Of other parts of the world he only knows that which his parents, hardened travelers, have recounted, and that which he has read in travel literature.

That youth could not revive a street in Vienna in his memory, and he knew that any invention, even though it was based on information from recent readings, would still be completely false. What really interests him, since he knows he will leave, is trying to discover what he could miss from his own country, once he has gone to another place. Against his back he feels the comfort of the easy chair he is sitting in, he breathes in the presence of the books (in part inherited from his father, in part inherited from Uncle Jacinto, in part his own), he turns his head towards where he knows he will encounter the desk, but he concludes that the affection he feels for this place has nothing to do with the city. He thinks that in Vienna everything could be the same and probably better; he could have a good library in any location.

Maybe the climate, which according to what some people say is much better than in other places? The mountains in the tropics have the advantage of eliminating the heat and humidity without reaching the level of snow and intense cold. There's plenty of sun throughout the year, and the downpours that flood the city are not problems that affect him personally. When he's away he won't miss the landslides that tumble the mountains of shacks and lean-tos that comprise the poor neighborhoods.

He could begin to feel nostalgia for the conversation of a few friends, when the rum still has flavor and hasn't yet made everyone drunk. The music of a friend who could pass the night singing. That youth sitting, immobile, is sure that he won't miss the scent of the guava when he's away, nor the dripping of water on the aluminum roofs, nor the interminable whistling of the cicadas in the countryside, nor the urban novels of the local writers that, as a friend says (whose sharp tongue he will undoubtedly miss), continue to stink like cow shit.

The young man that I was and that I see likes the leaves of the plantain plant, but the memory (although not very clear) will do; he won't go so far as to have nostalgia to return and see them with his own eyes. The national newspapers will make so little difference to him that he will forever fight with the person to whom it occurs to continue sending them to him, once he is away. It is said that ours is the best coffee in the world, but he, even then, drinks coffee, or tea, or chamomile tea, or blossom tea, or whatever, with indifference. Just as he is indifferent in his relationship with cocaine, which he tried only once imitating Sigmund, and with marijuana, which makes him very tired.

After thinking a lot about it he arrives at a conclusion: the only thing he will truly miss will be the language. The language of his childhood, the words of his friends, the language with which Eva Serrano revealed to him that he was rich and that it could be rich to kiss. The youth that I was, then, thinks that in Vienna he will continue to concern himself with his language: he will teach it or he will continue learning it, which is more or less the same thing, and now I realize that this is what I have been doing during these long decades of voluntary exile.

Is there then neither destiny nor chance, but choice? Some bearded man with glasses will have said that liberty is the choice of the necessary. I chose what I needed: to continue living in my language, for my language, fixed in that place which damaged Freud and which carried him to his tomb, which carried to the bonfire or the gallows such illustrious linguists as Giordano Bruno or the utopian More. *Yosoy tueres eles* (Iam youare heis), that will be what I will miss in Vienna—the language of Valdes and of Nebrija, of Don Andres and of Cuervo.

If the peninsulars left us something good, guilty of the counter-reformist and priestly slaughter that is my country, it was this instrument which serves us even to insult them, asshole (which is our homegrown form of saying your wanker), and to ascribe to them part of the blame for our disgraces. In any case the fates didn't carry me to Vienna nor return me to Medinaceli. They brought me to this Turin of wide avenues and narrow palaces, of a French "r" and good wine. And I am grateful that I never came to rest in Vienna, for I would never have been able to learn German. And I am also grateful (it's a saying, I'm not grateful to anybody, nor to the altar with one die which is the only chapel of my belief) to not have come to stay in Madrid, for with these manias of nobility, now, instead of remembering, I would be investigating in the archives of the whole peninsula, doing the impossible to discover a documentary aid that would allow me to request with pride a title of baron or viscount. And all for being the invented descendant of an Asturian chief—a very good subject of his majesty and of very clean blood—who was able to slaughter eighty-seven scared Indians during the Conquest.

Nine

In Which, While Pondering Names,
a Somnolent Incident Occurs.

J ACOBO, ANTONIO, JORGE, GASPAR. WHAT SHOULD YOU CALL
me? All of these names my father, Don Juan Esteban
Urdaneta, wanted to give me. Gregorio, Serafín, Elías,
Benjamín. What should you call me? All of these names my
mother, Doña Pilar Medina, wanted to give me. According
to an agreement in which my mother won by one name, the
Christian name on my extensive baptism certificate appears
thus: Jacobo Gregorio Benjamín Gaspar. But at home they
could never agree. My father preferred to call me Gaspar.
"Dear Gaspar" in his letters, Gaspar! when he called me upon
arriving home to show me the presents he had brought from
Peru. And my mother preferred to call me Gregorio; Gregorio
come here and Gregorio, are you there? And me? What do I
call myself? I would have chosen Serafín, because it's the
name which is most like me. But since it was one of the

discarded, I have ended up calling myself Gaspar, according to the wishes of my father. And to compensate I chose my mother's last name, Medina. Gaspar Medina. Is this my name? Well, yes, although I would never have started this chapter with "Call me Gaspar," like any gringo would. No, I have never been content with my name, but that's what you should call me, Gaspar Medina, just as it has remained written. Quitapesares' question, *What's in a name?*, is one of the queries which has most fascinated me. I believe that every person ends up encountering his secret and true name. And let me demonstrate that with an anec...

I have continued dictating for more than half an hour without realizing that my loyal secretary, Cunegunda Bonaventura, was no longer in this world. She was off extensively traversing the profound territories of sleep. Asleep on top of the papers, the pencil still in her hand, and that absent smile that she always wears while I dictate to her still on her lips. But she couldn't stand the stupor of my soporific explanations of names, and thus, for eternity, luminous pages about what dwells behind a name are lost. Oh Cunegunda, sleeping beauty, sleepy sleeper, some day this carelessness of yours will receive its just reward. But maybe I understand you. I have let myself talk like a book, I have lost the trail of telling stories and submerged myself more and more deeply in arid reflections.

So that you won't fall asleep, reader, so that Cunegunda won't fall asleep, I will stop digressing. Don't go, don't you all go. And don't you get distracted, copier of my tales. Now, with great regret, casting aside one of my firmest convictions, now something is going to happen.

Ten

Whose Protagonist is the Sacrament of Matrimony, with its Innumerable Possibilities & its Consummate Validity.

MAYBE LOVE CAN BE MISSING FROM A LIFE, BUT NOT FROM A book. Love is the salt of books, just as adultery is the salt of matrimony, matrimony is the salt of adultery, and salt is the salt of soup. For me, love has always been an exercise of the imagination, a spiritual game, a swelling of thought and not that twisting up of the innards nor that interchange of body fluids and exhalations of the flesh. Nor has it been that explosion of emphatic adjectives that the poets string together. I have never been able to say, definitively, like Melibea: "My trouble is in my heart, my left breast is its dwelling." Would that it were so. I have loved the search; I have loved love, that which doesn't exist. I never could, like others, clear the breach that exists between reality and desire, and, for eternity, the desolation of the chimera has overtaken me. I have cared more for the lip than the kiss, more for the gesture than the hand, more for the smile than the woman. And as these memoirs seem to have turned into a continuous present and not, as they should be, the entertainment of a soft old man remembering just how he is, I will announce that just a few moments ago, after 72 long years of bachelorhood, I have married.

Yes—what are you complaining about? Don't love stories usually end this way? Well, I am going to begin at the end: this morning I tied the sacred matrimonial knot with my unfaithful secretary. And as adultery is the salt of this bond, we will celebrate our honeymoon here, in this library, with a blue-eyed Indian chief (the son of my cook) as instrument of the caresses and delights of the nuptial chamber. I have set a feather mattress at my feet with mirrors at its head and foot so that I will not miss the details of the spectacle of my honey moon with a vicarious husband.

I should advise the reader of several things. If he is under age he won't be able to read this chapter without the danger of something being agitated in his loins. *Galeotto fu il libro e chi lo scrisse*. It's not clear exactly why, but there are fathers and mothers that detest and are terrified by the masturbation of their children. These moralistic dinosaurs know that all the world, and probably they as well, masturbate or have masturbated or will masturbate. But civil man is sneaky by nature. If this is the case with your parents, young reader, don't let them see this book, and don't tell them what you are reading. If they find you out, tell them that you have it for kindling. If the reader is an adult, be forewarned that here he will have to submit himself to seeing written that which he himself, whether he is normal or abnormal, has done while awake or dreamed while asleep (and vice versa). If he doesn't want to see written that which he does, and even less that which he dreams, he should skip this chapter or tear its pages out. If he is an abstemious person, possessor of a rigid sexual ethic, he should also follow the preceding instructions. Be advised. He who accuses me of pornography is admitting that he wanted to read the following, and therefore the pornography, after I had told him not to. No more hypocrisy: he who wants to read it goes ahead at his own risk and responsibility. He who doesn't, can skip ahead to the following chapter, for this story of beds adds or detracts little from my temperate and chaste life. I am the first to reduce the importance of the sex life. They have led us to believe that it is the source of everything; poppycock, it's mere carpentry, as Quitapesares says.

Miss Bonaventura—I don't know if I should call her Mrs. Medina—has been good to me, and she deserves everything. Not that a girl of her age could be happy to marry an old geezer like me, who on top of everything is sick. But actually it is this last detail which makes me a good choice. I will die, at the latest, the coming year. But it seemed bad to me to leave to the State (even worse—a First World State) my Italian possessions, my private old age pension, my life insurance, and it would be even worse to leave to my tide of Colombian cousins the acres of terrain in my motherland which I still control; those Americanized cousins of mine are already far too spoiled to need to have their presumptions augmented with the force of millions. My modest, chaste and humble Cunegunda will make better use of my parents' fortune.

Bonaventura, *Bonaventura bona*, good Bonaventura, blue cat's eyes, breasts of a young siren, hair of a Pre-Raphaelite virgin, upon my death and for the rest of your days you won't have to work again. Without lifting a finger, the fortune that I am leaving you will monthly render more, much much more, than that which is necessary for your own maintenance, your degenerate lover's maintenance, and that of all the *hidalgos* and chiefs that you want to acquire during the rest of your chaste existence. I know you have made a good deal, and I am going to die able to recount something more: that I have married. That I have arrived at nuptials with the delicious Cunegunda, she of the perfect tit, she of the most attractive belly, she of the best lap, she of the most lovely vulva, she of the enchanting hands, the luxuriant, plump and appetizing lover of this new and old Candide into which my days have converted me.

With me you won't have any descendants. You will know, Cunegunda, that the century was already well advanced when I read of a new invention: by eliminating or interrupting I don't know what microscopic activities, a man could free himself from the weight of his successors. That which my fellow men viewed as a humiliating half-castration was for me the resolution of a nightmare: having children; that a descendant of mine would arrive through trickery or careless-ness. I suffered this obsession quite possibly as an atonement for a sin of youthful pride. As I have already said, during several years vanity led me to effect exhausting and continu-ous (Monday, Wednesday and Friday) sperm donations. Too late I read that page of Quitapesares in which he denigrates mirrors and coitus, which reproduce men, and he convinced

me of the naïve and terrible vanity of heirs. This new conviction thus led me to always use double condoms during coitus;
I remember with pleasure the surprised look of the concu-
bines who shared my bed, upon seeing me slip on to my
member a second prophylactic over the initial one. And don't
believe that this precaution permitted me to freely discharge
my fluids inside that dark vessel, extremely welcoming as it
is, but unfortunately not always a semen-tery. My fears led
me to interrupt the embrace even while sporting the pair of
condoms. And what can I say of those interminable cleanings
of the private parts that I prescribed to my lovers, and of my
insistence on the abundant use of spermicidal creams? The
idea of having a child was the terror of my nights of insomnia. Until I received the news of that definitive operation
that was being performed in Houston. Within a few weeks I
was in Texas, on the waiting list, of course not very long, of
the first men who submitted to the experiment, already perfectly resolved and demonstrated in bulls, chimpanzees, rabbits and pigs. None of these animals, after the operation, had
lost its potency; but all had freed themselves from the useless
baggage of fertility. To me, truthfully, the very risk of impo-
tence had not preoccupied me in the least for, as I have
already said, I never tasted the delightful consequences of
priapic labors. I had consulted about it, and were it not for
related endocrinological problems I would have had no mis-
givings in imitating my uncle the archbishop's famous singing eunuch. I didn't do it because I didn't like the idea of
gaining weight like a young bull for the rest of my days nor
the image of converting myself into an obese, greasy, human
ox. I never understood why the saints of my church never got

around, as far as I know, to castrating themselves. As the Bible clearly says, if our right eye scandalizes us we should tear it out and throw it far away; I don't have to be Carl Jung to know that the eye and the phallus occupy the same house in the neighborhood of symbols. If you tear your eye out upon gazing at someone's ass, or you cut your hand off after caressing it, I don't see why you shouldn't uproot the famous witness that we are male and not female. The works of high poetry are impermeable to vulgarities, but in pedestrian language the verse would sound different. If your virility arises in the presence of someone other than your official woman (or in the presence of whomever, if you are married to the church), maul into a coffin your two balls. This is what the Scripture means to say (the Master or his scribe), as even the most obtuse student of hermeneutics clearly understands.

Overwhelmed by my hagiographic ignorance I have called my friend Quitapesares on the telephone. He has quoted Matthew, who says, "There are eunuchs who were born thus from their mother's bellies; and there are eunuchs who were castrated by men; and eunuchs that castrated themselves out of love for the kingdom of heaven." He has added that many doctors of the church have detained themselves over this and other biblical passages. Thus you can see that my interpretation of the sacred texts is not rash; the same conclusion was reached, for example, by Origines, a wise, beatified man and a martyr. This singular man, fed up with the anguish in which lust submerged him, had himself castrated. The Church, nevertheless, has always opposed this testicular mutilation and for that very reason, and only for that reason, has not made an official saint of this man who was as saintly, or more so, than many saints. Oh, Saint Origenes, patron saint of eunuchs, I invoke you and supplicate for your intervention so that my seed never escape from the dark and narrow caverns where I have it cloistered.

Yes, with this Voltairian Cunegunda I have contracted matrimony. So many times I could have done it, that of contracting, and not with her. With Eva Serrano, for example, with Catalina Mejias, with Susana Robledo, with Angela Pietragrua, with Josefina Logroño, with Matilde Sotomenor, with Artemisia Tomasinina, with Lorenza Battaglia, with Luisa Spiraglio....I had to take advantage of the opportunity to recount my incomplete sentimental education of failed love affairs. The story of Eva Serrano you already know and you also know that it relates purely to tongue. Catalina Mejias, in the best of my premarital euphoria, turned out to be a lesbian, like one of the protagonists of *Paraíso Perdido* by John Huecos, a local novel of civic customs. I was scorned with an ignominious and summary trial, just like that in the novel, and I don't repeat stories. Suffice it to say that for the mere offense of being a man, that is a *homo erectus* of the masculine gender, Catalina Mejias accused me of all faults and all crimes, except cattle rustling.

I don't know why I didn't marry Susana Robledo (the last descendant of Sir Jorge, conquistador of my lands). She was an excellent pianist with only one defect: she played the sonatas with her metronome set at too slow a rhythm; the *allegro assai* came out *lentissimo* and the *lentissimo* came out somniferous: a note every two seconds. She spoke the same way that she played: her quickest phrases were isolated words, between every term she made a pause and one had to always ask her what the punctuation was for what she was saying: "The other............... day............ I was............ in my house............ and............ it............ occurred............ to me.............. to................. call.................. on the............ telephone......." I was incapable of hearing whole stories; I have never been a rushed person, but her oral style demanded a very large concentration. At any rate, since she almost never spoke, this defect of Susana Robledo wasn't very noticeable. The truth is that she was slow in everything. When she showered it took her as long as it would take anyone else to take a full bath with a double change of the water. If she bathed she took the whole morning. Her pace when eating exasperated waiters. I, knowing her problem, took her to restaurants at eleven-thirty in the morning. But at twenty to four we still would not have been able to arrive at the desserts, and we had to go have coffee somewhere else if we didn't want them to physically throw us out. Her circumspection reached such extremes that on various occasions the stoplight turned red again without her, during the green, having had time to engage the car in first gear. And if I had decided to get married to her, I think the preparations for the wedding could have lasted until yesterday, so that the matter wouldn't have changed; marrying her or not marrying her would have had the same real result: this extended bachelorhood. The few occasions when we had enough time to get into bed, I began the preliminaries the eve before, in such a way that many hours later, when the sun came up, with the little man worn out from painful expectation, the act of unheard-of sluggishness finally culminated. But with the genital union finally crowned I had lost my capacity to contain myself, and her fury at my premature overflow was a disaster. Luckily there was plenty of time for a second attack, and once or twice I attained, sometime after midday, her arrival at the ecstasy of which others speak and which, for me—*ay*, it pains me to confess it—is only a relief, a rest, like urinating after having let your bladder inflate for a good long time.

I am becoming aware that I don't create accurate portraits but rather caricatures, but at any rate it's certain that my loves were superficial.

Not all of them. For Josefina Logroño, a bad-luck bitch, my last Colombian love, I think that I felt that which the nineteenth-century novels name *passion*. I think of her (during the time that we shared) and I still bite my lip with anger. Bits of spit from bad wrath flower in my mouth. Josefina Logroño, I hope you are rotting with your little husband, the dentist. He seduced her—but who will believe me—with the dull ambiance music of his office, dentist's music, you can just imagine: Beethoven for idiots and saccharin Bach, a Chopin made into Clayderman, electronic taffy. Well, all in all, this is the end of the story. Ah, but how much I liked her in the beginning, and right up until she got that damn abscess that was to be the cause of my misfortune.

Now I see clearly that she was just a high-class whore who in the illustrious dentist found someone to maintain her, thanks to the insuperable aroma of her pussy and the generous dimensions of her tits. But I am lying, the preceding is not true; my memory doesn't speak from the serenity of these days in which I scratch my ancient wounds, but the fury of those fateful days in which Josefina Logroño traded me for the dentist. It would be stupid to fall into the misogynistic consolation of converting into whores the women who embittered our existence. Besides which, judged honestly, Josefina elected that which most suited her.

At any rate, the infallible way to forget about an old love is not to remember it during the period when it was a good love. The best approach is to try and see that past object of desire again. That's what I did in this case.

The last time I saw Josefina Logroño was in her post-marriage house, the one the dentist made for her, and after several years of matrimony without children and with a puppy. I was in one of my periodic return voyages to the motherland and I remember that I called her on the telephone. The servant answered: "Residence of the illustrious dentist Don Aurelio Escovar." I was at the point of hanging up, still blind with rage, but now also with laughter; I managed to contain myself and asked her to let me speak with the dignified spouse of the illustrious dentist. She invited me to lunch. I arrived at noon and the first thing I noticed was that the house, like airport waiting rooms, was invaded by ambiance music; those dental melodies diffused through speakers hidden in every corner, from the bathroom to the trees in the yard.

In the yard, precisely in the yard, I encountered the Escovar Logroños. She was smoking a long mentholated cigarette, stretched out on a couch with a yellow plastic cover, and at the same time ecstatically observing the disgusting work which her consort was performing. I, who have never been fastidious or excessively scrupulous with my hygiene, was nauseated when the dentist stretched out his hand. I don't know if you will believe me, but I swear that the molar-puller was milking the dog. Yes, for the couple, instead of children, had a dog of I don't know what breed, who suffered from utopic pregnancies. After her heat, after her fruitless heat (for the couple submitted her to total abstinence), the poor hysterical dog convinced herself that, through some supernatural intervention (this I add from my mind), she was pregnant. And so pregnant that she began to produce milk. After a mastitis that brought her to the edge of the grave, the illustrious dentist had to milk his dog twice daily during the long weeks of her illusory lactation. So I discovered him, wrapped in music and splattered with pink canine milk when he held out his hand. I went to the bathroom to wash my hand, caught in the intolerable net of music.

Josefina, a bit rounded out after six arduous years of married life, offered me a whole pork loin (with the bone still in the middle) with potatoes *à la bogotána*. Eating flesh I looked at her flesh and everything about her reminded me of Bachue, the big-titted goddess. From the yard, and over the ambiance music and the moans of lactation of the hysterical dog, floated the oral babbling of an aphasic parrot who repeated *cacáo cacáo* throughout the whole meal. But the conversation at the table was no more illuminating than the parrot's until after the husband went off to his dentistry. Then Josefina offered me more meat, pork meat at first, and then her own meat, but by now I didn't really want any. Thus, between the husband's milk and the wife's ham, all wrapped in an insipid musical tissue, I cured myself of my last Colombian passion.

The farewell with which Josefina surprised me, nevertheless, was amusing and beautiful. After finding out that I no longer wanted to repeat the monster with two backs, she conducted me to the bedroom anyway. Behind her dresses she showed me the steel door of a safe and slowly she turned the knob, entering the combination; when the door opened, her trembling hand searched out a circuit breaker and she cut off, finally, finally, the dental harmonies. "It's been six years, Gaspar, six years now blanketed in this melody, but I almost never dare to turn it off. It's the price of my matrimony, and I pay it."

But she had not brought me there only for this. Her trembling hand entered again into the darkness of the safe and from it withdrew, with great care, an El Rey matchbox. She gave it to me and asked me to open it carefully. Inside the box there were a few curly hairs. Josefina said to me: "The last time that we did it (I knew that it would be the last time), when you left, I collected all the pubic hairs that our passion had disseminated across the sheets; they are my greatest treasure." I let loose one of the few guffaws of my life, but I shut up when I saw her eyes filling with tears and I was incapable of disclosing the thought that was making me laugh: That I had seen a lot of stupid things in my life but none quite as stupid as saving such stupidities.

Eventually I also fell in love (is the verb too strong?) with Italian, Scottish and Brazilian women. Here I should say that they are all the same. But they are all different; not one was similar to the other, each one distinct. The same in that, I must say, for men (and thus I complete another phrase for my collection of reversed clichés). With all of them, I think, I committed some error, of excess or in a simple defect. With Artemisia Tomasinina, for example, I was foolish enough not to take action in time. When I finally wanted to do something, we had already become friends and it was too late. Lots of brains, lots of talk and when I wanted to draw near to her lips, our minds got in the way. Not even my kiss could dampen her, not even her kiss could moisten me. If we like a woman we must not allow her to become too good a friend before we grab her breasts; there will be plenty of time for friendship, but we must start out listening to the body's reason which neither the head nor the heart can understand.

Love, love I felt, truly, only for Angela Pietragrua, my first Italian caprice. I was twenty-six when I met her, and she had a noble lover at her side. She worked at Einaudi, the Turin publisher, but in an administrative position, and for that reason neither Calvino nor Pavese had noticed her. Too bad for them—they will never know what they lost. She had the body of a fifteen-year-old and the stupendous face of twenty-five intensely lived years. Yellow eyes and dark brown hair in long curls, disorderly, almost always pulled back and held by a simple elastic. Long legs and an agreeable bust, perfect hands.

But my secretary says, or my wife Bonaventura, that it is not at all in good taste that the very same day of our matrimony I should set myself to write first of Robledo and Logroño and now of that woman that maybe I loved, Angela Pietragrua, and not of her, my only legitimate spouse. She is right. I ring the bell to call the adolescent that we have contracted especially to consummate our union. I am unable, or I don't want to, as I have already said, so we have hired the son of my chef, a blue-eyed chief, to calm the newlywed's impulses that my Cunegunda has, and to relieve my canonical qualms regarding that *ratus sed non consumatus* or however the hell it goes.

There enters the chief, already well-armed; he knows what we are calling him for. Wrapped in his underwear I note the swelling of that which resists remaining enclosed between his legs and behind his fly.

I receive the blank pages from the hands of my wife, and now I am charged with taking notes. The Sioux Jesus of the blue eyes is kissing her on the mouth. My wife Bonaventura doesn't refuse to open her lips. They surrender themselves to a linguistic sucking, like those that Eva Serrano applied to me… ah, they exchange saliva with a fury of noises, without that artificial chastity of the Tomasinina, my woman who never was. Now Jesus, with one hand, searches her back looking for the clasp of her blouse. He has turned skilled in the operation of undressing her, as now the first veil falls from the stolen bride. Underneath is the bodice that she has put on for the ceremony. My good woman must be impatient, for she has dropped her hand to the pubis of her vicarious husband. She lowers the zipper, slips her hand in, and it doesn't come out empty, she pulls it out with the excited mulatto penis between her fingers. They have gone horizontal on the soft mattress. He manages to free her from the fastidious bodice, and the perfect breasts of Cunegunda Bonaventura vibrate with the light that filters through the curtains. I see her breasts quiver and the mouth of the Indian takes possession of a part of her right tit. The hand of my wife continues in control of the full dick of my good servant. She caresses it with urgent insistence, she forms a ring with her smooth little hand and makes the skin of the dark indigenous member press against itself. He pulls up her skirt and pulls down her panties suddenly. The bright red pubic hair of my ward and woman appears, her extraordinary cunt is wet like a stormy ocean. I recite out loud to them an old ejaculatory poem: *Open your legs, young woman, you win more than you lose. Push, young man, you pull out more than you leave behind.* Wall Street would love the business of the nuptial chamber. While I recite with great spiritual absorption the nuptial prayer, the couple embraces, both of them agitated and trembling. Then I smile at them with paternal affection, and a strange fear crosses my spirit, wondering what in the future, of anguish and disillusion, the haste of the chief will save for her. And as though he had heard my premonition, what do I see? I see that the member, rubbed hard by that pale hand, is spitting out milk before its time, that the ineffable seed falls on to the belly of my shocked wife, that the blue-eyed boy groans with pleasure and shock, and that now my woman furiously protests and demands that my hand, at least, the hand that I gave her before the witnesses this very afternoon, make her feel, there, in her foamy vulva, the pleasure that the blue-eyed one hasn't been able to give her with his dark penis. Ah if I had fewer years and less ailments I would do it well, but like that maimed soldier of Urbino, I have more words than hands. In my state I can do nothing but write.

Eleven

Which is Occupied in Making a Repertoire of Bodily Noises.

CUNEGUNDA BONAVENTURA ASKS ME ON OUR WEDDING NIGHT, Why in my long existence have I never married? Will I make, finally, a pure confession? It is so simple and so dirty, and it explains so well the distortions of my mind…. But, finally, I will say: because of corporal noises. I never could endure the squeaking gamut of the bubbling of the body. I do not accept even the knocking of the pulse. That remote amniotic percussion (water clock of the body's blood) is for me the anguish of time's passage, a cruel clock, the unnecessary noise of the silent soul, disproof of the immutable spirit and affirmation of elapsation.

Additionally, while you hear this orderly palpitation, you can assume a sudden creaking of lower viscera. Base bubbling liquids that pass from one place to another, unexpected rhythms, intestines accommodated in the narrow space of the thoracic chest.

Not to mention the stridence of sneezes with their aerosol shower of saliva and germs. Or the convulsive blow of a cough with its hoarse climax in a splitting head cold. Or the sudden burst of a burp, a failed fart. Or the chaotic and secret rhythm of hiccups. Or the fetid shrapnel of inferior flatulence, posterior belching. Or the rasping of the muffled yawn. Or the strident whistle (from inside, from outside?) which at times overpowers the eardrums.

I remember that ever since I was a child I would shiver when those people blew their noses in Mass, or maybe during a reading of Isaacs in class. I was exasperated by those who would double over their fingers until they cracked with that conclusive protest of the bones. And the rusty machinery of the creaking knees. And the obstructed chimney of angina, and the sniffling of noses, and the heavy wheezing of the asthmatic, and the monotonous and voracious splatter of the suckling.

From the loudest, like the yearning puffing of tiredness or the suffocated panting of fright, to the lightest, the most subtle, which for that very reason captures our attention with greater tyranny, like the diminutive snapping of the eyelids (oh yes, you need a very fine ear to hear it), the intermittent opening and closing with a small blow that is neither liquid nor contusive. The voice, respiration, the spirit, ambushed by so many dissonances. By the noises that are dry, wet, thick, sharp, low, overwhelming. Like the jet of pee against the pool of the toilet, tiny waterfall with its final intermittent drops, when the sphincters drain the bladder, and everything ends in one drip, another drip (plas!), with the desperation of a badly closed faucet. Like the sonorous hysteria of sobs, the guttural noises, the sharp moans, the suction of the nose, the splashing pool of the eyes. And the snapping of the tongue to say no, and the resonant bellow of applause or the guttural applause of a bellow.

Except, maybe, the rumor of kisses. The sound of kisses over the skin of Angela Pietragrua (and over your skin as well, of course, Cunegunda) from the neck down to the buttocks. The murmur of the kisses on her lips or on my lips, the mouth held as a horn or a spout or a sucking trap, the horns which unite and suck and boom with that resonance that disquiets the whole body. Or that deaf murmur of the secretive kisses, when it seems that the soul (I don't know what it really is, a pit) shivers and emits an inaudible chirping, painful and heard only from the inside.

My science fiction, my dream of being an angel, has waited in vain for a magnificent operation that would strip me of this body, this animal. This is the dream: my head cut off (the rest of the body in a sty with the pigs) and machines and hoses to keep me alive, to sustain the silent activity of the brain, and nothing else. The dream of a pure soul (freed from desires, noises, needs) transformed by a rational science that doesn't believe in the soul, but only in gray matter as the source of all thought.

Twelve

A Narration of the Elegant Encounter with the Viscount of Alfaguara & his Beautiful Concubine.

THE IMPRESSION THAT I HAVE OF MYSELF AT TWENTY-EIGHT OR twenty-nine years of age, when I met Angela Pietragrua, is not very precise. It bothers me to remember people that I don't like, and the Gaspar Medina of those days I don't like. I had established myself in Turin just a little while before, and for the first time in my life I suffered a serious crisis of insecurity. Maybe it was the hasty circumstances of the voyage, a troubled flight more than a meditated decision; maybe it was my age, united with the feeling that I was nearing the halfway point of life and I still had defined nothing of my present or my future. I didn't have sufficient experience to define once and for all, definitively, that clarity doesn't exist and that the little that we are able to influence in our present and our future is very slippery. I have known boastful people, full of self-sufficiency, who describe their journey through existence as a series of realized efforts. Many of them are perfect loafers who haven't noticed it was pure luck that three consecutive times the dice came out sixes. But it is not chance that I want to talk about, but my desperate love for Angela Pietragrua.

At thirty my futile illusion was that of being able to unite completely and forever with Angela Pietragrua. But I look into the mirror of those days and I don't encounter in my aspect anything seductive; I look back and view the almost thirty insipid years I had passed with neither suffering nor glory. Although my pockets are full of dollars, I don't have a job that I can exhibit as a professional triumph. I have fallen into the machinery of merits and qualities and I see myself as an obtuse and sinister zero. When I see myself with Angela Pietragrua, who cares for me, I collapse into a marmalade of self-contempt. I erase myself, I sink into myself, I cancel myself.

In the days when I met her, I was a dog whipped by the latest events in that country of wolves where I had the amusing misfortune to be born. In April of '48 I was in Bogotá and I was, at the same time, a fresh-faced professor of Aesthetics and a false student in my next to last year of law school. My temperament free of violence and commotions, recalls with horror the assassination of Gaitan and the Bogotázo. But the truth is that history doesn't touch the perfect egoist; he passes impermeable through the world (or this is his illusion), immune to the incidents, always the same to himself, enraptured in the thawing of his cold soliloquy.

For this very reason I will not recount the months and decades of blood that followed that calamitous date, source of so many deaths. I leave the report of those events to History with a capital H, with all of its amalgam of truth and lies. Nor will I recount how I came to be in danger of being sent prematurely to that other world that doesn't exist. Let me just say that on Christmas Day in 1948, in Turbo, I embarked, incognito, on a banana boat that made a stop in Panama. With my trail of blows behind me and after a pilgrimage through Central America, Mexico and the United States, I arrived in Italy around the middle of '49. On the twelfth of January of 1950 I met Angela Pietragrua. Or was it the fifteenth of July of the following year? It seems like a lie, but now I can't remember.

It may have been in July, for I remember that I sweated as I climbed the ample stairway of the palace of the Viscount of Alfaguara. But it could also have been in January, as nobles are cold-blooded and they get used to keeping the heat going full blast. I climbed up, well, sweating, the ample stairway of the palace of the Viscount of Alfaguara; in my pocket palpitated a letter of recommendation for the Viscount in which the Cardinal Uzbizarreta, of Madrid, implored the gentleman that in some manner he harbor in Turin this unhappy Colombian refugee. The Viscount of Alfaguara received me with total indifference, without offering to shake my hand or rising from the papal chair behind his desk. With his hissing peninsular Spanish he told me that the only thing that he could have done for me was to name me tutor of his nephews, but unfortunately the indigenous accent of my Spanish prevented him from offering me that mercy. He could never permit that due to his fault and mine, in the future Courts (he said it this way), his relatives would be made fun of for having such a servile and plebeian accent from the Andean highlands. I answered his excellence that it was not a phonetic incapacitation that impeded me from pronouncing his *thetas* and his *thes*, removed the *pe* from *Septiembre*, the *de* from *Madri* or the *elye* from *Seviya*. That it also was not from laziness or ignorance that I resisted the use of *vosotros*, but simply because I did not want to use it, and that my aspirations were very far from the idea of being tutor and disciplinarian and coach to his dignified brother's offspring. That he should find himself some sick Castilian and all together they could put themselves, finally, in the same place whence their curses against the host and against ten were emitted ("I shit on the host," "I shit on ten"), but that I had not crossed the salty sea—in which he also defecated—to put up with such bullshit. I took a bow and I exited without another word. As the door to his office was closing behind my back, I heard him call out, "Medina, come here, I want to introduce you to a woman who enjoys snappy answers."

But I am lying. The old man who I am today has nothing in common with the youth I was then. The old man that I now am knows (and says) what that young man should have answered and was incapable of uttering. The old man that I now am would like to modify his past and who he was into a youth full of dignity and arrogance. But I cannot continue putting make-up on my memories. The Medina of those days should have been a dog, for he committed the weakness of not even answering. With his son-of-a-whore complex intact (which in vain his godfather tried to uproot), he lowered his eyes and in a low voice answered that, seeing as he couldn't serve as a tutor, he offered himself as a simple servant. Due to the kindness of Alfaguara, after fifteen minutes of conversation, he reached the high position of majordomo of the palace. The Viscount said, well, another phrase, very different from the one found above: "Well, Medina, the job of majordomo is yours. I would like to introduce you to a woman who appreciates humble and servile temperaments." He sounded a bell, and soon after, Angela Pietragrua, his concubine, appeared.

I can't remember any other woman that has made such a strong impression on me from the first encounter of our eyes. When I saw her I couldn't maintain eye contact with her gaze for more than an instant. I looked at her waist and her hands, but neither could I maintain my gaze in any part of her body. A painful current wrinkled my throat and I felt a kind of vacuum in my loins. If I lifted my eyes it was worse, because only listening to her I already knew that I was entirely in her hands and that I would do what she ordered forever.

Will I be capable of describing the woman of my life? Love, I believe does not have anything to do with the body, with skin color or with height. Factors which we don't understand intervene in the blinding glare of love at first sight. Angela Pietragrua had a clear and smooth voice, a slow way of moving, large hands and not so long hair. Bah, I am incapable of describing her, just as I wasn't even able to look at her. Love at first sight is blind, it does not look, it has no vision.

She, as if she had known me forever, began to speak to me in her language, in Italian, and maybe I recuperated a little, as I felt less feeble for an instant when we passed from

Castilian to Toscano. I had heard the Viscount direct comments to a waiter and I had been able to note that Alfaguara's double consonants were appalling, not to mention his chaotic conjugation of Italian verbs. Before Angela, although without looking at her, I was able to unfurl the virtues of an Italian spoken with an almost native accent.

But that hard-hearted noble did not let me enjoy this linguistic superiority either; with one lash of his tongue he declared that speaking without an accent in a foreign language was a sure sign of a cowardly character. And it was this, maybe, that was the original sin I was never able to atone for in Angela's eyes: in her eyes I was always a loser.

Thirteen

In Which Long and Disorderly Pages Are Dedicated to the Extraordinary Love for Angela Pietragrua.

BAH, POOH, GRRH, EECH, BURRR, ERRRG. GRUMBLING IN A book is ridiculous; you end up looking like a minor character in a B-movie. But sometimes the only thing you want to do is mutter angrily. And yet the onomatopoeias do not allow my secretary and wife to note down the eruptions of discontent that spurt from my mouth when I remember my first encounters with Angela Pietragrua, in those days when I was the Viscount of Alfaguara's ass-kisser. It's hard to record all of it. I am not a supporter of those Nobel Prize novels whose recipe consists of censuring the possibilities of written language. I don't share their visceral disdain for adverbs; or for the period or the comma, or for dashes or for the exclamation mark. The signs of writing are so few already that dispensing with them is only castrating yourself even more. And this despite the fact that in Spanish, you can still transcribe surprised questions: "¡What, you have named a young political refugee majordomo? What if he turns out to be a revolutionary!"

This is what Angela Pietragrua exclaimed or asked the Viscount of Alfaguara, her official lover, when he told her of my new position. I found myself obligated to explain with humility the terms of the letter of recommendation from Cardinal Uzbizarreta. It was not true that they were pursuing me as a dangerous character in my homeland. I humbled myself to the point of saying that it was misunderstandings, purely misunderstandings, that had obliged me to abandon the violent country of the dove.

It is difficult to understand my state of being then. I have said that the Medina of those days was a whipped dog, tail between his legs, without a bark and nothing but a yelper, never threatening to bite anyone. I had enough money to set up a house, buy an auto (as my lord obliged me to say, enraged by my South American 'cars'), and contract a Spanish majordomo. I could have invited Alfaguara to dine at my house with more than sixteen pieces of silver per diner (shit, what a chore!) and more exquisite plates than those of his palace. But I was a whipped dog and I wanted to feel like one. I served, I served, and while serving, I realized that it is more contemptible to be served than to serve. Thus, if they had named me the janitor in charge of cleaning the palace bathrooms, I would have accepted with infinite gratitude. I felt like the last of the mortals, and I wanted them to treat me as such. Now even the post of majordomo seemed to be a lofty privilege that I didn't deserve.

In that moment of dark depression I met Angela

Pietragrua, the only woman I have ever loved. To say it with a horrible phrase, I will say that she was a woman full of corporal perfections, it's true, but with a spirit or a soul (as I wouldn't have said even then) that made her deserving of all attentions and affections. Of her body I retain innocent alms-of-Mnemosyne memories, if you like: an Andalusian fan which ventilated August's drops of sweat upon her nose, a dimple lost somewhere in her face and the curve of her neck which became so disturbed when my breath ran along it. Her mouth humid from not speaking, against my lips, dry from talking. That's what I say (badly phrased) about the body. Of her soul, I can say that it had the insuperable quality of being full of books. Angela read day and night, she read like an obsessed woman, and her head was full of quotes and bookish characters. The aspect, the attitude, or the words of every person she encountered were memoranda from some work she had read. "Doesn't it seem to you, Rodrigo (that was the Viscount's Christian name), that the Countess Archibugi is identical to Madame Verdurin? Isn't it incredible how the majordomo seems to have been copied from a Walser novel?"

The history of my love for Angela Pietragrua is too long and tormented. To avoid making it the endless material of an entire book, I am going to limit myself to the essentials. I met her, well, from the most abject position that my interminable existence has known. The Viscount, a Phalangist with the look of a greasy butcher, had left his native Toledo during the days of the Civil War, as an Italian contact for the fascist militias that went to help Franco combat communism. And he had stayed in Turin, surrounded by a group that was nostalgic for the monarchy, and each day more mis-

erable in the face of electoral results that favored the repub-
lic. But who cares about this? The Viscount Rodrigo Alfaguara
was a shady fascist, that's all, and he treated Pietragrua like
his private whore and me like his favorite. In reality, we were
in similar conditions of slavery, with the difference being
that she also commanded me.

For many months our only contact was the typical hier-
archical exchange between master and servant. I responded
to the orders with obedience, to the scoldings with humility.
I did everything well and if occasionally I managed to commit errors in my duties, I think that I did it on purpose, for
in those days it would have pleased me to have the Viscount
beat me in front of Lady Angela. This only actually happened once, at the end of our acquaintance, when I had
exhausted my submission and at the same time let it reach is
fullest flowering.

As far as I know, it has been centuries since the Medinas
of my branch have served. The Viscount of Alfaguara was so
pleased with my performance that in a few months he had
augmented my salary twice. He didn't know, of course, that
my checking account was just as swollen as his. Nonetheless,
I accepted those raises which helped me distribute more money
among the servants of the palace. Somehow, from my first
day in the Alfaguara household, I knew that I should win
the favor of the servants, of my colleagues, oblige them
through prizes and presents to be my allies. Without pre-
meditating it, but already having a presentiment of it, I was
buying their complicity and their silence for the approaching romance. But I am getting ahead of myself.

Through the months during which I served, I asked myself why I wanted to continue serving. Nobody was obliging me to sleep in that cold room, next to the ancient coachhouse, on the most rickety cot that my back has ever known. There was no reason why I had to walk around all day dressed like a clown, with white gloves extending to my elbows, and a little black tie around my heavily starched collar. No necessity commanded me to go each day to the market in Porta Palazzo to do the shopping for the sumptuous feasts of my masters. But I came to realize that what had started as a game, or as a secret punishment, a sacrifice demanded by the cowardice of having fled my country in its worst moment, was converting itself more and more into an irrepressible desire to be close to, to be the servant, to be the slave, of Angela Pietragrua. Throughout a whole winter I pretended to please the Viscount and I bent over backwards for her without gaining the slightest closeness.

Finally, bit by bit, I don't know if it was with a pinch of intention or not, Angela Pietragrua, my mistress and my lady forever, began to commend to me more trustworthy tasks. At first these consisted only of taking her dresses out of the wardrobe, or preparing the water and the foams for her extended baths, but bit by bit, with a casual adjustment of the bodice or with the rapid closing of a zipper, my task began to convert itself into something more intimate. Since she pretended to treat me as a neutered chamber servant, I feigned knowing the art of combing hair, only for the pleasure of brushing her hair; I learned all about the skills of the pedicurist and manicurist, with the only goal being the privilege of caressing the callus-free feet and the spotless hands of Angela Pietragrua. I am sure that she was aware of my awkwardness with the file, but despite everything she continued calling me and I passed hours caressing her toes, putting creams and perfumes on them, dying inside for being unable to draw my ardent lips close to them. That bit about the ardent lips is tasteless, but I am leaving it because I am not speaking in metaphors: in the winter my lips were always burned by the cold.

Despite my ever more intimate duties, in those days I never managed to see her naked. In her underwear, in lingerie, yes, but not even veiled attractive lingerie, for they were bulky, chaste and not in the least bit transparent, garments.

Purely by accident I also became her secretary. One day she noticed, observing a shopping list, that my calligraphy was clear and correct. That same afternoon she called me to her desk and just as you right now, Bonaventura, transcribe my words, just that way, I began to copy down the delicate words of my owner and lady. Although if I think about it, it wasn't carelessly that she named me her amanuensis. In those days I didn't want to acknowledge that she made me her secretary so that she could dictate to me that which she couldn't say to me. Thus I came to learn about a few of her intimacies. Of a poor brother, for example, who lived in Lucca and to whom she sent a little bit of money when she was able to steal it away from the avaricious Alfaguara. I hardly need add that I augmented the quantities before closing the envelopes, and that my lady was surprised upon receiving the fervent letters of thanks from her brother. I also found out that everything wasn't roses in her relationship with the Viscount. Angela had a friend in another place, a Patrizia, if I remember correctly, to whom she wrote long letters when she was sad or in a bad mood. Pietragrua criticized the Viscount for his manner of speaking and she said to her friend, making fun of him, that he spoke like an antiquated book, that is to say, like an imbecile; instead of *horse* he said *steed*, instead of *letter*, *missive*, *rural property* or *rupestrian estate* instead of *country house*, and he called doctors, *physicians*. Thanks to Angela I learned not to envy the Castilian of the Viscount and I think that these notes that she made in her letters were an indirect message to me; as if she wanted to console me for not having been given the job as tutor of the illustrious nephews because of my Castilian. She dictated everything to me, without the slightest reserve, with less bashfulness than she would have felt seated in front of a typewriter or a tape recorder, with less shame than that which I feel before my wife Bonaventura when I dictate to her about Pietragrua. So I knew about the Viscount's hurried habits in bed, of his scarce generosity in questions of money, of his immeasurable jealousy and of how he harried her with it, rummaging in her drawers, opening letters, throwing open doors, and interrogating her for hours about the precise direction of her gaze.

How I loved the imperative tone of her contralto voice: "Gaspar, I have to dictate some letters; come to my office at two-thirty." And once we were seated there she started without delay: "City and date dear Patrizia finally Rodrigo has left and I can hasten to recount to you the latest news last night we were in the house of the Marquesa Oddone de Bligny and as usual Rodrigo drank too much which means that upon our return there was a quick embrace on the living room sofa and so it went he had that horrible breath from

drinking coffee after dinner and not brushing his teeth..."
Until she arrived at farewells and kisses, and said "another
city and date dear brother only to tell you that I received
your letter and I don't know what you are talking about for I
only sent you a few lire of course the most that I could at the
moment," et cetera. She insisted that all of her letters must
be written in sepia-colored ink.

The Viscount, in his function as procurer for the peninsular nobility, was obliged to make numerous journeys throughout Italy and pass extended periods in other parts of Europe.
When her lover was away on long voyages, Angela dressed
as a widow, completely in black right down to her calves, a
veil covering her face and an embroidered mantilla over her
hair. This seemed to me to be a highly flirtatious detail,
almost an announcement to all of her admirers that finally
she would be alone for a few days, but through one of the
letters I discovered that it was the Viscount's order, he dreamed
thus of avoiding all intentions of treachery.

When she was in mourning, she invited me to her room
and before the lit fireplace asked me to read books to her. I
chose my fatherland's few worthy authors (in those days)
and she laughed with Efraén's untenable indecision, with
Maria's candor ("I don't know a woman who is less like me,"
she said to me), with the voyages of that one who gambled
his heart on chance and lost it in the jungle, with the chivalrous descriptions of wide Castile ("I like his Spain more
than the one Rodrigo describes to me," she said), with the
thankless mornings in the villages of Antioquia and the pure
and archaic language of the characters of Sir Tomás
Carrasquilla. I read until I lost my voice, but she always

remained thirsty for letters.

During one of these mournful voyages, after a passionate reading of the harmonic verses of de Greiff, Angela called me to her side. She said that since I knew so many useful things I would surely also know how to give massages; that the departure of the Viscount had made her nervous, the muscles of her neck and back were stiff, her tendons were strained and knotted. And as she communicated her ailments to me she gradually stripped herself of her dark veils. Without uncovering her legs she undressed herself from the waist up, but I wasn't able to catch even a glimpse of her breasts since she was facing away from me and she immediately stretched out face down on her bed. She indicated to me where the cream for massages was, in a little box in her desk, and I trembling, began to execute the sweet new duty of caressing her back. After an initial timid approximation, she asked for more force, "Harder, Gaspar, at this rate you will leave me worse than when you started!" I don't know where I found the power and the daring to climb onto her rounded gluteals. I sat on her buttocks and with the cream I began to massage the most perfect back that my memory recalls.

My wife Cunegunda is not jealous, as the Viscount of Alfaguara was with his concubine. But she has turned pale upon noting my enthusiasm for that distant massage from over forty years ago. She has gotten up and left me here, a crowd of words in my mouth, papers scattered on the floor, ink spilled. I have collected the pages and I am forced to continue alone, without dictating, dictating directly from my head to my hand.

Angela Pietragrua trembled without saying a word when I seated myself upon her precious buttocks. With all the strength in my arms I began—from her neck down—to knead concentric circles across her back. From her mouth, every now and then, spasmodic moans, almost censured, allowed themselves to be heard. I worked in silence, pressing only very lightly with my buttocks over hers, but with a slow and prolonged rhythmic movement. After a few moments of astonished delight, I heard her say, "Yes, yes, Gaspar, that is much better, you could earn much more as a masseuse than as a butler, you can go." I climbed down off that body which for the first time had lain under mine.

Many lies seem to be accumulating in this book of memories. Maybe the greatest of them is my claim to total indifference before affairs of the flesh. But it is not a lie. In reality it is only a general rule. With its exception, which was Angela Pietragrua. Excepting, possibly, the first kiss of Eva Serrano, my relations with Angela Pietragrua are the only which permit me to understand men's sexual excesses. But my chaste indifference, along with my general distance from everything sentimental, is truly my ordinary life, in these final days and throughout the great majority of the twenty-six thousand five hundred and seventy-four preceding days. Love, as well as desire, has been a parenthesis for me, unrelated to the rest of my life; caprices of the epidermis or sudden quiverings of that metaphor-charged viscera. My heart, as though it were the spring in a watch, seems to wind itself at times and mark a break in the natural course and the tedious character of my daily existence. But let me return to my story, to my parenthesis of love, to readings and desire with Angela Pietragrua.

After this first massage my nights and my dreams, my sleeplessness and my vigils, were converted into a torment; sudden cold sweats, stubborn binding of the lower parts, run-away imagination and the impossibility of acting. Three days passed, with their respective nights, before Angela Pietragrua again called me into her presence, and not for a letter or a poem, not for a broken fingernail, a drawn curtain or a stuck zipper.

She said "Once again, Gaspar, my back is tense, come to my room at three, well-rested, to give me a long massage." As a trivial lover's strategy, I, who have always been scrupu-lously punctual even down to the second, arrived in her room at a quarter after three. In her face I saw repressed fury, but for the first time since I had entered her house she was humble just as I had always been. Upon seeing me enter she pointed out the box of cream and she began to remove, with extreme languor, her multiple veils, all of them the color of dark night. For the first time she didn't turn her back as she un-dressed and suddenly, after a few slow movements, the white full-moon of one of her breasts appeared. A second moon appeared, quivering; all of the veils fell, down to her waist. It was a fulminant and instantaneous apparition, for immedi-ately she was extended on her bed, with her back turned towards me. This time I didn't want to sit on top of her. From the edge of the mattress, and without her commenting either positively or negatively, I began my work. After a few minutes I heard her whisper, "The legs also, also the legs." With great delicacy I lowered the slip and the wide knickers (which they used in those days) that covered them. Thighs and calves appeared that should only exist in Plato's heaven.

I anointed both extremities with cream, forcefully, until I was almost sweating over her. Then I conjectured that maybe her buttocks could be considered part of her legs, and I tried to introduce a hand under her panties, my smeared hand moved towards her bottom. Her imperative voice detained me: "Not there! You can go."

The return of the Viscount was expected the following morning. On the last night of mourning I myself took responsibility for conveying the supper trays to the lady's table. I had them prepare seafood dishes, little samples of an infinity of fish and shellfish, mollusks reminiscent of women. Many times, in the end, I filled her goblet with a white wine from the cask, that Sauterne of Proustian memory, which she drank with relish. During coffee she told me that yet again she had begun to feel a certain tension in her neck. She didn't demand it, it didn't form part of my ordinary tasks, it was not my obligation, nor did she want to tire me with her whining, but couldn't I, just this once, repeat the massage? *"Ma certo, signora, alle diece?"* (Why certainly, my lady. At ten?) "Yes, ten would be perfect."

This time I was punctual, and exactly at ten I again entered her bedroom. I found her stretched out in her bed, under the eiderdown which was pulled right up to her chin. She maintained the ritual of pointing out the box to me, and she turned halfway over under the covers. I asked permission to lower them a bit and I began to notice, inch by inch, that she was completely naked. Again I climbed astride her, this time onto her thighs, and as I inclined my torso over her to massage the high part of her neck, I could draw my nose and mouth close to the nape of her neck. It was on this occasion that I perceived with clarity for the first time the natural odor of Angela Pietragrua, a scent that would continue to persecute me for years and years, and that even today, at times, during the desolate winter afternoons, I can recapture in a secret garment that I conserve in the deepest corner of my great-grandparents' wardrobe. It was an odor completely her own, I don't know how to express it, but to give you an idea, I would say that vanilla was one of its elements. She felt my breath's voracious rhythm and she augmented the pace of her respiration. I was dressed in very light white cotton clothing and my sweat made the fabric stick to my skin, but I didn't dare even roll up the sleeves of my shirt. I mastered with my two hands, completely, each one of her posterior parts. She permitted me to spread a bit of cream down the perfect crease which divided her two cheeks, and I actually went so far as to touch with my index finger the clear little pink button, only just insinuated. She also sweated, but she didn't turn over, she didn't speak to me, she didn't moan, she didn't say anything until the morning. When the sun began to show us its light through the curtains, I thought, noting her perfect tranquility and her peaceful respiration, that she was profoundly asleep. It was then that I dared to kiss her neck and I realized that the sleeping beauty was very much awake. Immediately, almost trembling, she told me that it was time for me to go and rest. I obeyed.

Yesterday I left my work at the preceding point. Today, luckily, I again have here, sitting on my knees, my faithful wife and secretary Cunegunda Bonaventura. She arrives at a good hour to note down that on the day after my complete night with Angela, soon after his arrival, the Viscount of

Alfaguara had me summoned to his study. He was irate, and an electric current ran up and down my spinal column when he began to speak, beside himself, "You, Medina, are an unsurpassed hypocrite!" I feared that one of the servants (despite the generous perquisites proportioned) had mentioned something about my repeated visits to the bedroom of his concubine and I lowered my eyes, preparing myself for the worst. He surprised me, for a change, with the obvious: "I met with Cardinal Uzbizarreta, in Madrid, and I looked like an imbecile when I revealed, planning to offer him my appreciation, that I had his recommended candidate as my majordomo. Astonished, the Cardinal told me the truth about your origin and status. I don't know why you have wanted to trick me during these months, Medina; in any case get out of here. You have half an hour to abandon my house, you wretch." Thinking of his avarice, I told him that since there wasn't just cause for my dismissal, he should pay me, in addition to the salary he owed me, an appropriate compensation. He need not rush to prepare it, as I had no urgency, but the following day without fail I would pass by to pick it up. While I mentally divided my earnings among the other servants, I went to pack my bags and I had a taxi called. Before leaving I announced at the top of my voice that if anyone needed me for anything they could locate me at the Hotel Principe. It was the best hotel in Turin; one night there was equivalent to fifteen days of my salary as majordomo. Undoubtedly, today's Gaspar would have found a more elegant response to the situation, but we will leave it as it is, just as I acted it.

Upon hearing the shout containing the name of the hotel, the Viscount called me again into his office and, without the mediation of a single word, in the presence of Angela, he slapped me. In other times the defense of my honor would have obliged me to challenge him to a duel. But the one-who-I-was limited himself to smiling, then I turned halfway around and walked out of the study for the final time.

I managed to hear the guffaw of Angela Pietragrua, and the incomprehensible howls of a Viscount beside himself with rage. I wasn't really too sure if Angela was laughing at him or at me, but in any case the misunderstanding left the noble in a worse position than the servant, and I think she enjoyed the idea that her lustful masseur had turned out to be the sole heir to one of the largest fortunes of the West Indies, as Uzbizarreta, exaggerating, had exclaimed.

That same night she called me at the hotel and delivered me from my doubts. With mischievous words she pretended to scold me for having tricked her and especially for having tricked the poor Viscount. There was a certain change in her tone of voice, but I enjoyed the detail that, despite the new circumstances, she hadn't begun to act too familiar with me. This was something very beautiful about my relationship with Pietragrua: until the unfortunate date of our definitive parting and even during our most intimate moments, we always addressed each other formally. I can also affirm that she never desisted from using the imperative verb form with which she had become accustomed to addressing me, and I also appreciated that. Even the last phrase that I heard from her mouth, when we said farewell, was an imperative, but that time I did not obey her.

So that night, on the telephone, she told me that she

was sorry that the Viscount had thrown me out of the house
for she was more than satisfied with my services. In fact, if I
wished to continue carrying out a few of my tasks, I could
tell her and she would try to arrange it. I told her that the
most rewarding functions I performed in her house were those
of pedicurist and masseur to the lady; if she wished to continue receiving my humble services, she should tell me the
time and the location in which we could do so. She asked
me if I rejected the old function of reader and secretary, for it
also seemed to her that I fulfilled these necessities very well.
I accepted the offer to continue being her amanuensis, but
no longer a reader of Colombian novels, as I had run through
the full repertoire of decent works. She told me that I must
know that her dependent economic situation impeded her
from paying me as would have been her desire. I clarified for
her that I could not do anything for free, but that I would
content myself with a symbolic fee, always and only if it
came from her hands. And thus we arrived at an arrange-
ment.

For all of those months I continued living in the Hotel
Principe, but Angela, well-known person that she was, could
not come there for me to offer her my services, for the gossips would have begun to murmur. We found a little two-bit
hotel near the Porta Nuova station and almost every day, at
unexpected and always varying hours which she communicated to me over the telephone, we met there. During the
first visits she didn't want massages or foot treatments. I had
to limit myself to sustaining her hands in mine, to covering
them with cream and to feigning that I was filing her nails.

But after I had obtained a new and decent mattress, sheets

of batiste (even today I don't know what it is, but she requested just this genus), and an eiderdown that was bigger and of a purer feather than that of the palace of Alfaguara, she acceded to undress and show me her back, her thighs, and her buttocks, for daily massages. I won't speak of my wakeful nights, my lower pains from the unbearable negative force of abstinence, my now explicit moans when I was with her, but she made it clear that she didn't want to go any further, or at least not prematurely.

Occasionally the Viscount's journeys granted us greater liberty, or at least, more time. Don Rodrigo's monarchic dreams took him frequently to Rome, where the heir, who sooner or later his Excellency would restore to the throne in Spain, lived. During one of her protector's voyages, the day arrived when Angela permitted me to caress the front of her body. The down of her pubis in the middle of her body, her navel barely insinuated, her tits which previously I could just barely catch a glimpse of, her mouth half-open and wet, with her tongue that traveled over her lips red but free of makeup, her yellow eyes which looked at me full of... Of whatever, of what the reader wants. My hands could journey over her from top to bottom, inside and outside, from the back and from the front. Nor could she stop me from letting my mouth kiss her, and I feel that my lips made a nest in her mouth, they ran over her body with a crazy lust (I am speaking like a Quitapesares) and they kissed each of her folds full of lukewarm aroma, and the rigid pink points of her breasts. The only thing which she didn't allow me to do was to undress.

Otherwise she also began to investigate my body with

her hands and I can swear that she didn't even detain herself before my most outstanding parts. I remember her lips which passed or posed over my erect member. There she touched and kissed (through the pants, which I had ordered sewn from thinner and thinner fabrics) with an impetus and a pressure which I have never seen again in any woman, there I actually wet myself, with a certain sadness upon noting that humidity which I would have preferred to decant in another location. Yes, in that place which also produced humidity, between her legs. Well, I drank there, I sucked there, I entered with my fingers and my tongue, with my wrist and my nose and my lips and my chin, with anything but that... which according to ancestral customs should enter there.

But I am running way ahead. To reach the preceding I endured months of inches of skin won, daily battles to take the fortress of the left ear lobe, to lightly touch the right nipple, to take it fully into the anxious concavity of my hand, to afterwards win it with lips, tongue, and teeth. Days of patient siege were necessary to be able to draw my mouth close to the down of her center, my fingers to the slightly parted little lips, my tongue to that opening which day by day was preparing to better receive me. And we could also fall back into old prohibitions which suddenly extended the forbidden zones of her body.

Once, during a whole week, she didn't permit me to even touch her lightly with my fingertips. It happened during a different journey of the Viscount, this time a longer one. It was a time of prohibitions, but also of liberty, which permitted us a fleeting test of cohabitation, a species of ephemeral matrimony suspended in a terrain perfectly balanced some-where between the spirit and the flesh.

Several months had passed since the embarrassing dis-missal from his house, when the jealous but, for vanity, con-fident Viscount of Alfaguara found himself obliged to return for several weeks to Madrid. Angela dressed herself in mourn-ing, and made an immediate appointment in the two-bit hotel of where we lived our good life. She ordered me to obtain a country house, immediately, and that same after-noon I had acquired, without seeing it, the vicar's house in Pulignano, of which I have already spoken at some point. It was an old house, made of stone, with a chapel connected to it, surrounded by an abandoned cemetery, sterile vineyards, near the twisted trunks of century old olive trees. In the sweet Tuscan hills, with a view of towers, of villas, and of the half-golden half-green curves of the Arno where Manzoni washed—in public—his dirty Lombard rags.

There, in that house of my evanescent nuptials, there is a tower with a wooden confessional stowed in one corner and a kneeling stool destroyed by termites. From that very spot I have dictated a part of these memoirs and it was there, on my knees that I dictated to Pietragrua my most ardent and devoted orations. It's curious, it's like a vengeance of paganism, that the best of my life has been erected upon the ruins and the disasters of fallen Christian precincts.

I had the few pieces of furniture that are necessary for a couple sent to the house, two servants and a cook who would clean and prepare to receive us went as well. The house was semi-decrepit, the roof full of leaks, the doors ridden with holes which the wind whistled through, the wood floor moth-eaten, the yard invaded by brambly underbrush and tall shrubs full of prehistoric spines, the chapel vacant, the remainder of its frescos eaten away by humidity and its altar demolished, taken over by spider's webs. The branches were barren of grapes and the olive trees boasted few olives. But there elapsed the three weeks that, if I'm not mistaken, justify my seventy two years of existence.

Angela had imposed an iron rule for the first seven days of our stay. We could not exchange a single word. Nor could we touch. By the force of gestures and implied understandings, by the simple act of looking into one another's eyes or at any part of the body (well, we could be naked) we would do everything. The servants were ordered to be as discreet as possible. At certain established hours they should leave the food, certainly or not so certainly very frugal, in the shabby dining room of the house. They must clean and prepare the bedrooms according to very rigid schedules.

The second week, according to the rule imposed by Angela, we could communicate in writing, with little slips of paper, and she would start anew not to dictate letters but to actually write them to me, this time for me, completely for me, and one following another, in such a way that I could perceive her sudden changes of humor, her ambivalent emotions for this majordomo and heir from the Indies. We could not speak even one word, we could not touch yet, but I could also write her letters, messages, petitions. I don't remember what I wrote her. I only know that we accumulated mountains of pages covered with scribbles, I know that I wrote six hundred and fourteen anagrams of her name, but we couldn't save even the trace of one lonely paper from those days, for the final pact was to throw into the Arno, on the day of our return, all of the messages that we had exchanged. From those three weeks which I can't forget I carry the incurable habit of dictating instead of writing. To write is a gallant trade; one dictates to create literature. There, I also contracted the vice of being a Lothario of letters, one who loves women by writing.

The third week we opened to the spoken word and to bodily contact. We could speak, tell each other everything, touch each other everywhere, do everything except penetrate each other. I say penetrate each other because at this advanced stage I had lost my identity as the penetrator. Penetration was the part, a subaltern part of union which was missing, and by now I didn't know to whom corresponded the realization of this act, if it was through her permission or through my imposition.

How much we looked at one another during the first week of perfect silence! How much we wrote to each other during the second week! I have never spoken as much nor touched as much as during the third week of words and contact. In the last days, it was painful to not be in contact at least with a millimeter of some part of her skin. We were incapable of disjoining ourselves, of detaching ourselves. Not being thigh to thigh or cheek to cheek or tongue to tongue or mouth to cunt or at least finger to finger, produced a sort of unbearable and aching crisis of abstinence. And we said everything to each other, we recounted everything, we recapitulated her life and my life until both of our memories seemed to become only one memory. And the love which we declared appeared unique. I almost do not know how to explain it, I was suffocated, it was like Dante's pilgrimage through hell, purgatory and heaven.

Three weeks later, with the date of the return of the Viscount approaching, we had to return to Turin. He, in reality, had returned earlier than planned, and thanks to paid informants he was aware of our retreat in Tuscany. The day after our homecoming, Angela announced to me that the Viscount knew everything, and not only that, but desperate, he had asked her to marry him and go with him to live in Toledo, where he wanted to establish his home. While she recounted all of this she excited me enough that I tore off my shirt and pants. I traced all of her body with my body, she kissed me and also drank all of my fluids, but she didn't permit my inflamed rascal to penetrate the flesh which, humid and open, she offered between her legs. For a moment I considered committing a violent act which until that day had never passed through my mind, but I rejected the idea as something unworthy of such a low-class nobleman and such a high-class concubine.

Days of incertitude followed. She loved me, but she had resolved to go to Toledo with Alfaguara. Do not ask me why, for that is something that nobody knows, and only the tortured hearts of a few women and even fewer men will comprehend it. We saw each other to cry together and afterwards to reenact our incomplete, or more complete than any, lovemaking. We decided that if she went, it would be definitive. I would not follow her to Toledo, we would never write, we would return to the same silence we shared before we met one another.

The last time that we saw each other, she came directly

to the Hotel Principe, late at night. That same morning she was leaving for Spain with Alfaguara. Her desire, now I know it, her visit, was an entreaty that I kidnap her, that I save her from the claws of the Viscount.

She knew that only I could make her happy, and that I would only be happy with her—that the happiness of each of us in this life depended on both of us, on our staying together. She, as the writer Quitapesares once explained to me, understood that, upon leaving me, she would kill me and she would leave herself ruined. She understood as well that the Viscount was a contemptible man and she knew that she herself didn't love him in the least. Why then did she go? Quitapesares responds that because—despite every-thing—she had decided to. And why didn't I hold her back? For the same reason, which it seems, according to Quitapesares, is a general rule in love.

We undressed for the last time and climbed into the bed. After we had hugged one another and touched one another and possessed one another on the outside as always, she asked me, finally, to penetrate her. This was the clue, the symbol of escape, of surrender, and now I understand it. But I refused to enter her body. I caressed with my erect penis her belly, her downy hair, her vaginal lips, but I refused to enter inside her. She was leaving that morning, and I thought that if I entered I would never return to reality, I would remain an-chored forever in the memory of her. She thought that if I entered her, she would not leave. She had wanted us to save that last element missing for a definitive union for only this moment, the moment of her decision to leave with me and begin our elopement. She wanted to make her decision to stay with me in the same moment that we tasted the forbidden fruit. I did not understand. I don't know if she understood that I had not understood. Or if she understood everything more fully than me. Many times during that early morning she begged me, she ordered me, to penetrate her. I, for the first time, did not obey her.

Fourteen

Which Tenderly Discusses
the Slaves of Domestic Service.

THERE WAS SOMETHING THAT I KNEW ABOUT MYSELF, BUT I didn't know how to describe it until I read Quitapesares, and I realized that trait could be portrayed exactly with his nineteenth-century phrasing. The centuries have changed but not the circumstances. He was an almost noble revolutionary among the bourgeois and I have been an almost bourgeois revolutionary among the poor. Yet again I exaggerate. I have never been a revolutionary. Nothing is so distant from my constitution as the activism and violence necessary for a rebellious temperament. I am anything but a zealot. But the inconformity that I have felt witnessing the stupidity and indifference of the members of my class, have led me to set myself—in my mind, sirs, in my mind—on the side of the poor. By the way, let me not forget to recount my expulsion from the Brelan Club, the headquarters of the my hometown's oligarchy. But I'll leave that for another chapter. Because in this one I must confess that in any case I—and here comes Quitapesares—have never been able to put up with the poor in close quarters. He states it thus, and I feel the same way:

"I would do anything for the happiness of the common people, but I would rather, I believe, spend fifteen days of the month in jail than have to live with the rabble. I must confess that despite my perfectly and profoundly republican opinions, my parents transmitted to me their aristocratic and reserved tastes. I abhor the plebeian (when I have to deal with it), and at the same time, calling them the people, I passionately desire their happiness. My friends, or those who claim to be my friends, use this to put into doubt my sincere liberalism. Everything dirty horrifies me and the common people, in my eyes, are always dirty." With one exception, of mine, the servant girls. They have been my direct contact with the poor. I loved them, and I love them, and I remember them, my slaves who believed themselves employees. Let me describe Tata, the oldest of them.

Tata was a little girl. No. For me applying the phrase 'little girl' to Tata is an act of faith in which I can only pretend to believe, at heart I am convinced that she was always between seventy and ninety years old. In any case, it was recounted in my house that Tata was an abandoned child who had begun working in my maternal great-grandparents' house before my grandmother was married. Maybe in those days the word servant made some sense: the orphanage of the nuns of charity decided, after a more or less substantial donation, that the best destiny for the young orphan was to entrust her to the care of a wealthy family where she would be provided with a mattress, food, rigid hours and a series of tasks.

Tata—in those days she was still called Sixta Sanchez—for years helped carry the buckets of hot water to the bathtub where Miss Constanza, my grandmother, made her weekly bath of boiling water, milk of a recently pregnant donkey, and various herbs. Sixta would have been about twenty years old when she received the order to follow Miss Constanza, now Mrs. Constanza, to her new home. My great-grandfather was a pious and upright man, president of the conservative directorate, the honorary consul of Spain and the author of charming narratives. Maybe he even perceived that the disorderly youth of Sixta could be a perfidious temptation for his firstborn, who was already destined, according to paternal will, to hear the supernatural call of a priestly vocation. At any rate, the fact is that Sixta abandoned the house as part of my grandmother Constanza's dowry.

Sixta would have been twenty-seven or twenty-eight years old when my mother and Aunt Marujita began to call her Tata (that was not an alteration of Sixta, but the nickname which hid a third pathway between mama and papa) and I must have come to know her in the middle of the Twenties, applying the analysis of reason, when she would have passed the threshold of seventy. She worked six months in my house and six months in Aunt Marujita's house, as she had been nursemaid to both of them, and they fought over her. I came to know her very well, during the six months of every year that she passed in my house and every Wednesday throughout the year when I went to eat and recite the rosary in Aunt Marujita's house.

Tata always had a candle lit to Saint Martin of Porres. She was black, just as he was, although maybe she had more Indian blood because she was thin and short and she had straight black hair. When I made her acquaintance her hair was no longer so black, but it reached down to her waist and she sat out in the courtyard so that it would dry in the sun. Then she would make a bun loaded with hairpins.

She slept in a room separated from the rest of the house, superior in rank to those of the other servant girls, submerged amidst gray trunks filled with secrets and broken tricycles. The room smelled of those biscuits they call ladyfingers, muscatel wine, and raisins. When I was ill, Tata made me baths of cornstarch, she rubbed my back with alcohol and she read me the heart-rending tale of Genevieve of Brabante because, according to Tata, in the tears that poured forth the evil humors exited the body. Each day she was deafer and a few years before her death they operated on her for cataracts. When she read me Genevieve she saw with both eyes, but she would employ an enormous magnifying glass which the Archbishop, my uncle, had given her before my birth.

I seem to see her, sitting in the sun in the courtyard. She is slowly removing the kernels, with her hands twisted from arthritis, from a tender corncob. In that distant late afternoon of my memory Tata is already completely deaf, but she continues to carry in her ear or in her hand (as though it were an earring or a cane) the ancient acoustic cornet or ear trumpet for the deaf that my mother had bought her in Vienna, from the most famous otolaryngologist of central Europe. Many years have passed since she could read Genevieve to me, for I see one of her eye sockets is vacant and I know that with the other eye she manages to distinguish silhouettes, the shadows of objects, and sources of light. When they operated on her cataracts the eye became infected and they had to remove it. Afterwards they operated on her other eye, which did not get infected, but neither did it improve very much; thus she had to walk very slowly, stretching her arms before her. She continued using, nonetheless, the pair of thick spectacles for farsightedness and the archbishop's magnifying glass. When I close my eyes I can see her: she is over eighty years old and she insists on working, on "doing her chores," as she says. We buy tender corn, beans in their pods, green peas, vegetables that she can recognize tactually and with which she instinctively knows what to do.

My mother has put the blackboard I once played school with in Tata's room so she can communicate with her. With white chalk she writes messages to her that have to be very short due to the scale of the letters. For her to recognize them, each letter must be as large as an adult's face. "TATA, HOW DO YOU FEEL TODAY?" my mother draws more than writes on the blackboard. And Tata responds, fine, dear girl, hearing a little more and seeing a little bit better although still not everything. She called my mother "dear girl," even though she was now over fifty. During the last two years Tata, every morning, continued answering that she was fine, even though my mother knew that she had slept very little or not at all, doubled up by that pain in her stomach which she sometimes spoke of out loud when she thought she was alone. "TATA TODAY I WILL TAKE YOU TO THE DOCTOR."

The doctor that she takes her to is a sweet old man who is surprised that Tata, at that age, can seem to be much older than she actually is. After examining her he speaks with my mother and he describes the most tragic situation without losing his sense of humor: "It is an incipient stomach cancer. Tata seems to be a one hundred and ten year old woman, and in the elderly even illnesses go slowly. Let's see which arrives first: old age or the disease. But sincerely it doesn't seem possible to me that she could endure this cancer." At any rate my mother begins to cry.

Tata yet lives a pair of Januarys, drawing close to ninety, without the cancer advancing sufficiently to kill her. Right up until a week before dying, she continues to work. Each day she eats less; weeks go by with water and a few table-spoons of white rice. Only the last week does she remain in bed unable to get up. She enters into a tranquil lethargy from which the only thing she accepts, strictly, is water. Early one morning, with my mother at her side, she stops breathing and the doctor comes to write the death certificate. Even at this tragic moment he doesn't lose his good humor: "She starved to death," he pronounces. My mother cries, afflicted: "She served us for almost eighty years and she would not let me care for her for even one week."

A burial in the family's mausoleum San Pablo's cemetery was decided upon. He-who-I-was was touched by our family's attachment to the servant class. The passing years have lead me to read books which recount that the Pharaohs had their dogs and servants buried with them; my ideas of those days have become more lucid and my tears more bitter.

I also remember my family's indignation at the homily offered at Tata's funeral. It is offered by an angry, modern priest. Like a fury he scolds my mother and Aunt Marujita;

he confuses us with the memory of my grandmother now dead for many years, with the memory of my great-grandparents now dead for more than half a century. He becomes furious with the whole family, children, grandchildren, and great-grandchildren who received all of the care and affection of Sixta Sanchez, the servant, for a bit less than a century. We look at him, disconcerted, asking ourselves if this intermediary of the Lord really has the voice of the Eternal Father. His sermon is a furious admonition against us, the masters, which excludes neither the eye of the needle quote, nor the list of beatitudes of the poor.

Now, I believe I understand the fury of that little modernist priest, which not one of my relatives was able to comprehend. The priest, like almost all leftists, could have been right, but he also had very bad taste. And what he didn't like was that all of those children of that dead nursemaid, instead of having a wreath of flowers made for her in the best funerary florist in the city, arrived bearing bouquets of flowers in their arms. For me, for all of us, it was obvious that flowers cut from the garden of the house were a more important homage than that of great wreaths full of ribbons inscribed with names and surnames. But the little priest, with his bad taste and his lack of education, thought that my family had not ordered wreaths to save money on the servant. His rage is against those unpurchased flowers, which seemed too humble to him.

Sixta, my great-grandparents' maid, supplementary dowry of my grandmother Constanza, nursemaid of my uncles and my mother, my nursemaid, our slave until eight days before she died. Perhaps in the future there will be no more Tatas, this abusive injustice of giving your own life to others. Does it serve as a defense to contend that we never took her gift for granted or that my mother suffered more with Tata's death than with the death of my grandmother? No, love of the slave doesn't excuse the owner, nor does this recollection which I will carry with me until the end of my days.

I also remember Adela the ironer, who came to the house twice a week: once to prepare our clothes and the other time to put the linens in order. She starched the sheets and my father's collars all morning long in enormous steel cauldrons full of paste. That creaking of the white sheets as I rolled into bed is a lullaby that I have never heard again.

Adela the ironer had a daughter, Marisol, who turned out scatterbrained. Marisol, when she was seventeen years old, escaped with a man. She returned two years later with a full belly, and Adela the ironer received her happily. She gave birth to a handsome and robust boy. She was still breast feeding the boy when she ran off with another man. For three years she didn't return, send a message or a letter. Then again she arrived with a swollen abdomen. Adela the ironer received her jubilantly. This time she gave birth to a baby girl, blond and precious, who looked like a little gringa. A year later, Marisol escapes again, with another guy. She leaves her mother to deal with the two little ones. Marisol seems more reasonable and during this absence she has her tubes tied, she already has sufficient children for when she feels ready to raise them. Adela the ironer, meanwhile, is unable to manage. She works in various houses, but collar by collar she can't keep up with maintaining the children, paying for their shoes, buying them food, paying the neighbor to take care of them while she works... There are American couples who traverse the neighborhood in search of children, they have contacts to rapidly facilitate the adoption papers.

Full of doubts, drawing advice from poverty and desperation, lacking news of her daughter Marisol (soon she will return with more children, she has been away for three years now), Adela the ironer gives in. The children leave with a Canadian couple. Marisol returns eight months later, alone, with an empty womb, abandoned by the last partner. Now she will dedicate herself to the children whom she can no longer replace. Adela the ironer shows her a Christmas card. Merry Christmas it says, and in the photo appear two very well-dressed children, covered with red clothing, skis on their feet, standing in the snow. Year after year, at Christmastime, they continue to receive photos of the children who grow up, so rich and healthy that they "seem like masters," says Marisol. The cards do not bear a return address; only the postmark and the Canadian stamps of the queen of the empire reveal from whence they come.

Romualdo, the gardener, was the thirteenth of his mother's twenty-two pregnancies. We were not suspicious in the Thirties, or we were too far from Vienna, for we did not understand and were exasperated, in the house, by an aggressive phobia which Romualdo suffered: he could not see a pregnant woman without becoming infuriated and spitting on the ground. I recall the pregnancy of one of my aunts, my father's sister, who came to work in our sewing room once a week on Thursday afternoons. During the six months when her pregnancy was visible, every Thursday afternoon Romualdo would hide in his little room at the back of the house, irate. At times you could even hear him vomiting. But in my house, we were not very shrewd, we didn't understand why.

Romualdo was, in everything, an exceptional man. He played classical guitar and *vallenato*—a local music—on the accordion. After having completed the maintenance of the grounds, in the serene nights, from the dark garden, the sounds of his chords drifted into the house. It seems incredible, but Romualdo introduced me to the notes of some of the fantasies of Fernando Sor. He didn't play them well, I now know, and his guitar was a cheap and rough instrument made in Marinilla, but the notes followed the score with a certain fidelity.

When he was in a good mood he got out his accordion. This was long before the folks from the coast, under an influence from Bogotá, made the *vallenato* fashionable. But even then my father, when he heard Romualdo, was delighted, and he didn't know why, he said, by that savage music with long phrases.

Romualdo cared for the dogs and he cut the grass, he pruned the rosebushes and he fertilized the aromatic herbs. One day he didn't return from his Sunday break. And we never found him or saw him again. He vanished. A few said that they had killed him with machete blows; others that he had returned to the remote coastal town where he was born; others that he had fallen and drowned in the Medellín River. In one of my houses in Antioquia his Marinilla guitar and his *vallenato* accordion still await him. And additionally in one of my political speeches, that maybe one day I will recount to you, Cunegunda, I proposed a measure in honor of Romualdo's judicious phobia: the prohibition of the public circulation of pregnant women, whose sight, I sustained, constitutes an appalling example for the common people.

Manuelita, Benilda, and Tomasa were the daughters of Rosaura and Feliciano, the majordomos of my uncle's estate near Amalfi. Rosaura Marin Bernal had married, with the dispensation of the bishop, her first cousin, Feliciano Bernal Marin. Tomasa was delighted to announce that she was named Tomasa Maria Bernal-Marin Marin-Bernal. The three of them were very close in age and they seemed like triplets; they were so white that in the town they were called 'glass-o'-milk', "here come 'glass-o'-milk'," and they had a certain ancient Christian peasant pride that you can find only in contemporary Antioquia and in seventeenth-century Spain. Feliciano and Rosaura sent them, one by one, to my house, when they turned sixteen. They departed the precinct of Amalfi, where they had grown up without ever traveling for fifteen years, and they came to serve in Medellín. Lady Pilar Medina had the reputation of being a good mistress and they came here to grow.

The first to arrive was Manuelita, who spoke an antique Castilian, very pure, and who had an enormous resistance to learning the Anglo-Spanish with which we expressed ourselves in my house. The first week she communicated to my mother that she was returning to her town for she would never be able to learn all of those names: *suich, closet, osterizer, barbiquiu, amplifier*... She was going crazy, at night she would go to sleep with a buzzing in her cerebrum. Never in her life had she ridden in a car, and she was terrified when she had to climb into my father's car on the weekends, to go to the country house. She squeezed into the last corner of the back seat, tense and trembling like a puppy. But Manuelita was an intelligent woman, and in a little more than a month she

learned everything. My parent's house was never better orga-
nized than when Manuelita worked with us.

Then Tomasa arrived. As initially there were too many
women in my house, my mother diverted her to the house of
some relatives. But Tomasa became ill. Her fingers turned
purple, her respiration was shallow, and she couldn't work
although she tried and tried until she fell down exhausted.
Our relatives returned her to us like a damaged appliance.
My mother took her to the doctor. After a badly treated
throat infection, she had gotten a rheumatic fever which had
affected her heart valves. They had to operate or she would
die. The Bernal-Marin Marin-Bernals had a very rare blood
type with a negative factor. Brothers, parents, and cousins
had to come from Amalfi to the cardiovascular unit to do-
nate blood. Tomasa was cured within a few months, and for
all I know she is still washing clothes and scrubbing floors in
some rich people's house in Medellín.

Benilda was the last to arrive and she had the good or
bad luck of acquiring a boyfriend. She got pregnant, gave
birth to twins, and soon had to leave. My father found her
work as a cleaning lady in a bank and I never heard anything
more about her.

But for a large part of my childhood, Manuelita, Tomasa,
and Benilda, the daughters of the majordomos of Amalfi,
worked together in my house; and from them, from Tata,
from Adela, from my cook Rosario and from many others
that I do not mention, I learned pain and tenderness, clean-
liness and determination. I understood, more than anything,
injustice. And I retain such a deep affection for the poor,
that now it will not go away.

Fifteen

In Which the Memory, In Memorial,

Insists on Remembering the Ineffable

Angela Pietragrua.

I F I BELIEVED IN FREE WILL, IF I COULD TRUST THAT THE COURSE of our existence was dependent on our actions, I would say that I committed the error of my life, one which would never again permit me to be happy. "Two did not marry, since then they live a reciprocal widowhood." This is Quitapesares's phrase which hammers me in the head every time I recall Angela Pietragrua.

Now she is dead. She died in childbirth, a few years after our farewell, in a public hospital in Toledo, to which the Viscount had taken her to save money. In any case, since I am infertile by my own choice, I never would have been able to lead Angela to die in childbirth. If our separation saved us both from disillusionment, her death has saved her in my memory from any corruption. It impedes me from correcting her image, from erasing the happy afternoons in which the hours passed away as we put into contact all of the centimeters of our bodies, except for a few.

In the four years that followed our farewell, until her death, our glances never crossed again, never did we write one line or send a single message. I was in Toledo, she was in Florence and in Turin, but we did not look for one another. I heard about her marriage to Alfaguara, almost a year after his trip to Spain, by pure coincidence. I was in the salon, having my many hairs of those days cut, and the barber, to distract me, passed me one of those silly magazines which are filled with the gossip of the stage and the chronicles of high society. The barber sensed the trembling of my head and he asked me if I felt sick.

Angela Pietragrua smiled, the white veil lifted, at the side of the Viscount of Alfaguara. At the foot of the picture was inscribed the place and the luxury of the wedding. Behind the couple there was a blond girl running. Nothing more. I can only say that the bride, in the photo, had the aspect and the candor of a well-educated youth, of those who are capable of submitting themselves to any torture to prevent their mothers from being displeased.

Angela knew that I had retired completely from worldly clamor. For four years, until her death, I did everything possible to convert my love for her into self-love, without achieving it. I practiced, as the Pythagoreans counseled, total retreat, absolute silence. If I could not speak with her, it was better not to speak with anybody. If I could not touch her, it was better not to touch anybody. I isolated myself, I lived alone, remote, in perfect silence. A sinister aspiration to asceticism reduced me to this shadow of a man into which I

wanted to transform myself. A man who doesn't feel. It was
then that I passed more time in that abandoned hermitage in
Pulignano, in that lost country house in the Tuscan hills,
that since those distant years has been the place of refuge
and salvation for all of my sorrows.

An obsessive recurrent dream repeated itself during almost all of the weeks of the years of my voluntary retirement.
I presented myself in Toledo, but everything impeded me
from entering the house of Angela and the Viscount. Guards,
police, fences, bars, normal people, armed people. An insur-
mountable wall separated me from her. At the end the Viscount went away on a journey and she, in mourning, came
out on to the balcony and called out to me, she admitted me
into the courtyard of her house through a secret door; white
sheets and shorn braids lowered down to lift me, as in stories
and romances, from the courtyard up to her window. I managed to enter through the window and I began to give her
the customary ritual massage and this time, after a few moments, she let me do what in reality we had never done: she
let me penetrate her. We made love in every possible manner
and I felt this unspeakable pleasure which reality had never
presented. Everything seemed to be perfect, as in heaven,
every desire or thought immediately converted into reality.
My mouth ran over her breasts until I was delirious and I
introduced myself completely into her body, which received
me whole. Suddenly, in the very moment of mutual orgasm
(for in the dream I felt mine and hers at the same time, I was
him and her and both of them together), everything col-
lapsed. I did not wake up, but I noticed that due to some dark
trick my sperm, in reality, had exited my scepter outside of

her. I had the terrible sensation that yet again the act had not been completely realized. From the glimpse of a total union I came out to a new rupture and from the one that we had been, again came two. Somehow I perceived, in the ultimate instant, that Angela had not let herself be possessed. The separation, at dawn, was painful.

In one of those absurd twists of dreams she had to awaken very rapidly, in the early morning, for she had to go to Einaudi, the publisher where she worked; and she began to dress hurriedly. I then put some music on and it was a Mozart aria, completely inopportune, that one which starts, *Madamina, il catalogo e questo / delle belle che amo il padron mio*. She coldly bid me farewell and she had only just left the room as I ran to the mirror to look at myself: I was missing an eye, like that Blas de Lezo of Obregon, or actually the eye was almost completely closed and consisted of nothing but white (on other occasions I saw that I had a nauseating sty).

This dream of momentary union and bliss, followed by sudden and successive anguish, invaded my nights during those four years of my retreat in Italy in the first years of the decade of the fifties. Upon waking, the sensation that everything I had dreamed in the dream was somehow reality, would fill me with anxiety. It was obvious that Angela despised me; for my cowardice, for my inopportune arias, for my white eye. Many times I listened to that passage of Don Giovanni in which Leporello concludes *Voi sapete quel che fa / voi sapete quel che fa*.

They were years during which the planes of reality and the imagination mingled for me and there were always invasions of one by the other. I was obsessed by the vanilla scent of Angela Pietragrua, and with my eyes closed I was able to retrieve it completely. And I felt just the same way about the texture of her skin, the cushioned firmness of her breasts, the hot and sticky heat of her winking vagina. Week after week, as in a private mass, I repeated the gestures, the food, the silences or the written words which we had shared in the paradisiacal days we had lived.

I never had a love that was so complicated and spectacular, and also, on top of it all, so completely imaginary. I didn't search for her, I didn't write to her. Or, more precisely, I didn't send her the interminable encyclicals in which I described again, step by step, the most minimal episodes of our brief idyll. I maintained that love alive through the effort of a meticulous recall of every one of the minutes passed at her side. And she was there, only a few hours away by plane or train. Instead of going for her I passed my days and months writing letters that were never sent or dreaming of complete unions that were never achieved. In one manner or another I declared my love for her on every page. But it didn't seem clear, or well phrased, and I had the certitude that she would not understand or believe me until I could encounter the right words to make her understand.

I don't know if during this time she was going through the same thing, if she had comparable dreams. I don't know anything, nor is there anyone alive to ask. I know that since those dates, I have not been able to liberate myself from a certain predilection for the retired life. I also know that it was then that these blue circles appeared under my eyes; they have not abandoned me since. Even today, when I see them in the mirror, I remember that they are the unconfessable

scar of my extraordinary love for Angela Pietragrua, and that
sacred origin (we lovers are so tasteless) makes me love them,
not as the defect which they are, but as if they were my best
attribute.

Just as nothing disproves the being whom we create in
our minds, there is nothing we love as much as something
which does not exist; we can accommodate it to our changes,
we can adapt it to every new dawn. It is their silence which
makes the mystics attentive to God. Don't speak, disappear,
and you will be indispensable, unforgettable. All of our attention is capable of being occupied by an absence. Write
nothing to him, you don't want to see him again (you don't
even let yourself be seen by him!) and from faraway he will
be faithful to you until the end of time.

This sudden and definitive silence of Pietragrua's was my
destruction, for it made my love perpetual. Luckily friends
exist. Yes, for Quitapesares, my beloved friend, told me that
between ourselves and a ruined love we must erect new actions, even if it is a broken limb. Neither four years of isolation nor Angela's death were enough to cure me; I had to
break a leg. It seems like a lie that a casual and clumsy fall,
though very painful, would have pulled me from desolation.
Many things happened in only a few days, after I became
aware of Angela's death.

I was still in the hospital when I was invited to compete
in an examination for a professorship in Spanish Literature
at the University of Turin. A fulminating heart attack had
ended the life of the young scholar, who had not had time to
leave behind pupils or to designate heirs. My four years of
isolation (years during which I barely read) had helped me

gain a reputation as an erudite man and Einaudi, thanks to the friends left behind at the publisher by Angela, had recently published a collection of my old essays on the double scatology of Quevedo, the metaphysical and the defecatory. I presented myself for the examination still wearing the cast and I think it was this visual impact, more than my poor qualifications, which convinced the jurors to offer me the position.

I found myself suddenly with my beloved several feet under the ground in Spain, and with a professorship on the same terrain. If I were a believer, I would think it a supernatural intervention of my muse from the heights. My professional life, in Italy and in the world, had resolved itself from one day to another, as though through magic. But this was not the triumph I was searching for and awaiting. The day after being offered the professorship I renounced the position due to my health. In vain various university commissions journeyed to Pulignano to entreat me to expel such an insanity from my mind. Nobody understood that I was in mourning for Angela's death and for the necessary death of my love for Angela. I did not want to leave my stupor and, now that I think about it, I believe that since then I have not lived anything but the shock at having loved so, and having had to stop loving the only woman who stirred my existence.

Sixteen

Wherein It is Revealed Who Was the First Victim of the Spanish Civil War & a Prayer is Recited for Don Rafael Pombo's Poor Little Old Lady.

N O PSYCHIATRIST HAS BEEN CAPABLE OF CONVINCING ME OF the damage my mother produced in me, or of the problems that I developed as a consequence of my father's errors. Despite the insistence of many therapists that I focus on this or that incident, I was never able to blame my parents for anything, except, maybe, for having let themselves die young and at the same time. I was sixteen years old and I was still in high school. They had been traveling through Europe and its peripheries for several months. On the night of July 18 of 1936 they were shot to death by unidentified persons in a hotel in Casablanca. At least that's what it said in the telegram that we received on the nineteenth, where it informed us, additionally, that since there was no Colombian consulate in that port, and due to the circumstances of disturbance of the moment, their bodies would be buried in a common grave in that distant protectorate. The money which my parents had deposited in the hotel was sufficient for this purpose. That was all of it. And that remained all of it. More than ten years passed before I was able to travel to Morocco, and neither footprints nor memories of my parents remained; they were canceled out completely by years of war and abandonment.

On the nineteenth of July of 1936, a Colombian—me—was the first orphan of the Spanish Civil War. A sad and rich orphan who was still more than four years from reaching majority. I almost never remember dates, they don't even matter to me, but I guard in my memory that which was, maybe, the great rupture in my youth. For many months I roamed among the houses of my innumerable uncles, while they remained incapable of agreeing on who should care for the little orphan. I didn't feel an inclination towards any of them, and despite the fact that in all the houses (maybe to seduce me) they treated me like a king, I only thought about returning to my room in my parents' house. I was saved from the guardianship of my uncles, and from my own ruin, by the rivalries between them and by the shrewdness of the Archbishop and the predilection which he felt towards me. By then retired and blind, he was living out his last years, and all of the other uncles (including those from my father's side) conceded him a certain authority. He, who with the passage of the years had become completely disinterested in financial affairs, became aware of the voracity of my relatives—for all of them fought to offer me their care as long as they were also consigned the administration of the estate. The Archbishop, upon seeing so many vultures, decided to convene a family council that would supervise and verify the progress of my instruction. For this purpose they would call fortnightly meetings at which I would be present to summarize my activities. He also named an administrator of the assets, completely unrelated to either of the families, whose performance would be judged by the same council of uncles until I reached the age of twenty-one.

The administrator was an unctuous and prudent old man, timid and honest like no other. The Archbishop, who for the past twenty years had been his useless confessor, had these facts very clear. And thus it was that even many years after my attainment of legal adulthood this punctilious bookkeeper made himself responsible for noting every dollar and every cent which came or went from my patrimony. In the family we granted him the flavorful nickname "The Insipid One," and since then, when I have had to choose an administrator, I have always done it by electing individuals who seem to be cut from the same cloth. This has been my only financial talent.

The Insipid One was paid a laughable sum each month, and each month he presented impeccable balance sheets which my uncles were obliged to approve, with only a few criticisms (to which the bookkeeper was immune) about the better investments which could be made with this capital by incurring only a bit more risk. But in this the administrator was intransigent; his investments were extremely cautious, and although the performance was not the most spectacular, year after year my patrimony conserved and augmented itself. My uncles, noting that they couldn't gain any fiscal advantage from my holdings, gradually left me, with my fortune, more and more alone, and I was able to complete my youth as I wished. Thanks to those prudent and meticulous administrators I have been able to live ever since with my consciousness liberated from any practical preoccupation.

When I finished high school, two years after my parents had died, I decided to take a sabbatical. I wanted to rest for a year, not to think more carefully about what profession to choose, as I told them to justify myself, but simply to do nothing; for one year not to do what it occurred to professors that I should do. I will not recount here the scandal and the fuss that was kicked up at the fortnightly family meeting when I communicated my decision. For the first few minutes they looked around perplexed, the majority of them had never heard the word *sabbatical* which I had just finished pronouncing (and learning while flipping through the dictionary). Uncle Justo, the frankest of them, later confessed to me that upon hearing that word he had thought that, as odd as that nephew of his was, he was surely converting to Judaism. When I explained more fully that for one year I was thinking of resting, traveling and meditating on the future, they screamed to high heaven. The Archbishop had died by then and the Monsignor was not present. Only Aunt Julia defended me, not out of goodness, as I originally thought, but because she hated me so much and was convinced that this path would precipitate my definitive perdition. Using caustic phrases and raising her voice higher than any of the men present, she silenced all of them in the name of liberty and independence. Her exaggeration was even greater than mine. Soon after I understood her true motives, and since then I am convinced that many of those who wish to cause us harm, when they get their way, don't know the great favor they have done us.

The uncles could have forbidden me that sabbatical year when I was seventeen. They could have compelled me to choose between law, engineering, and medicine, the only acceptable professions in those days for men of my class. But for little Aunt Julia, liberty was the only path that led to the precipice; and she wanted the precipice for me. She chose liberty to drown me, and she saved me, or at least she gave me the opportunity to continue constructing my life as I wished.

I had resolved, should the opposition of my uncles be too overwhelming, to enroll myself in law school. I doubted profoundly that they would permit me the imagined sabbatical, but everything was facilitated by the sudden and unexpected death of my grandmother. I am noticing that there is another gap in my memories; so far I have not said anything about my grandparents. This may be due to the fact that I was able to get to know only one of them, my father's mother. The other three were already dead when I was born.

What can I say about Blanca Calderon, widow of Urdaneta? She seemed to have been made in the image of the poor little old lady of Rafael Pombo. Avaricious, plaintive, perpetually preoccupied by her imagined ailments, by the extinction of her wealth, by the nonexistent caprices of tropical weather. She had six children (to whom she gave birth, it's true, but who were raised by Mincha the black wetnurse) and I don't know how many grandchildren. Despite her numerous progeny she lived alone in the same mansion in El Poblado where my father and my uncles had grown up. She complained of loneliness, but she didn't invite anyone over. If one of her children or grandchildren came to visit, from the moment they entered the house she advised them that she could not invite them to eat because they had not warned her of their visit with enough anticipation. And if someone notified her in advance, and from Monday announced, "Grandmother, on Thursday I will come over to eat," she would respond, "Ah, we'll see, Thursday is a long way off." Then she would begin complaining of her lack of visitors all over again.

I remember that in those first days of my awareness, it must have been at the party celebrating my first communion, she gave me a very nice gift, an expensive toy train. From that day on, and for the following thirteen years, until her death, every time that she saw me she remembered the present. "Do you remember the train I gave you?" I swear that if the damn train had not been worn out by that time I would have returned it to her.

When her youngest child, my father, died, her greatest preoccupation was that it not occur to them to put the surviving grandchild in her care. She lavished kisses on my cheeks, she told me how much she wished she could take me to live with her in her house, but it was not possible, it was complicated; she had space, she could not deny it, but with more people in the house, the servants would get tired and would leave her unattended. There was never affection in her voice, she dedicated all the caring she was capable of mustering to herself. She protested, she was surprised by her solitude, without noticing that she estranged herself from any human contact, any company.

She had never needed to lift a finger, nor had she discovered any task, useful or useless, for herself, not even the most vapid. Grandfather Urdaneta had always treated her like a queen, and nonetheless she felt herself, throughout this time, to be bored and tired. She had grand illusions, she believed she was of better stock than anyone else in her family, and more noble than her few friends, who also abandoned her one by one.

She reached the inevitable destiny of those who never have cared for anyone—nobody wanted her. She died, finally, when nobody expected it anymore, from old age. For decades she had been announcing her approaching demise, and like the sheep who cried wolf, when she actually became sick, nobody believed it. She called her five children again and again on the telephone, to tell them that she was having trouble breathing. Each of them told her that they would stop by to see her immediately, but they didn't even really consider leaving their offices or their houses. Clinging to the telephone, with her voice weaker and weaker due to the asphyxia, she was dying. She expired with the mouthpiece in her hand, without anybody believing the telephonic death rasp. When Camila, the housekeeper, called to say that she had died, my uncles could barely believe it. "It can't be," "Are you sure?" "What did you say?" were the recurring responses. The very same Aunt Julia, when she finally arrived at the dead woman's mansion, began to note that something was moving behind Grandmother's eyelids and she tried to convince her brothers that it must be a case of apparent death. The brothers were too busy taking inventory of Grandmother's possessions to pay any attention to her. By this time, even in a case of absolute catalepsy, they would have decided to bury her alive.

They were filling notebooks with the detailed descriptions of paintings, tapestries, furniture, vases, jewelry. Treasures accumulated over the course of a life of avarice, of which each brother would now try to acquire the best slice. Since my father had died, I was due a sixth of my grandmother's legacy. I saw in this fortuitous situation the opportunity to peacefully earn my sabbatical year, buying it at the price of my inheritance. Deliberately making a fool of myself, I claimed the leftovers of the distribution on the condition that they would let me decide how to manage my own life.

I was one of the few grandchildren who attended the burial of Doña Blanca Calderon widow of Urdaneta, my illustrious grandmother. It was the driest funeral I have ever seen. Not one of the children shed a single tear or eulogized her with an agreeable memory. The parish priest tried to move us with a canonical sermon about our debts to her, with trite and classic similes about maternity, but it was useless. He spoke of Lady Blanca's laborious life, of her dedication to her house and her children, of generosity and of the vigilant filial love. He spoke of the anguish, of the desolation in which the children found themselves after such a grave, a truly irreparable, loss. But not even all of her children were in the church. Aunt Ana had come from Santa Marta to help compile the inventory of the possessions (her sneaky brothers weren't going to swindle her), but due to unavoidable commitments she had to return to the Coast that same morning. Uncle Pedro had awoken with a high fever, and the doctor had prescribed rest. Aunt Julia had a migraine and had to leave, precisely at the hour of the funeral, to see her therapist so he could treat her with a "laying on" of the hands. Aunt Amalia, Uncle Juan Gustavo and I, representing my father, remained in attendance.

Upon leaving the cemetery Aunt Amalia and Uncle Juan Gustavo were discussing how much time would be necessary for putrefaction (two, three years) to be able to liberate the tomb and stop paying the expensive rental of the alcove at the cemetery.

It was after this funeral that I decided to change my surname. It seemed better to leave the lineage of the Urdaneta, at least my branch, liquidated. I knew that my father had never felt close to his family, and for that reason his memory did not give me pangs of conscience. I wanted to close, at least with a symbol, my relationship with this band of heartless peddlers. Without telling anybody I began to sign "Medina," my second surname, and even though that foreign surname still assaults me upon opening my passport, I escaped introducing myself linked to the scheming of the sordid Urdanetas.

Seventeen

A Dictation Which Reflects

on Astrology, a Modernist Poet,

& an Abominable Adolescent.

LET ME TRY TO START AGAIN IN AN ORDERLY WAY, IN THE STYLE of David Copperfield, to see if I finally understand: I was born in Medellín (let us suppose that it was at midnight under a full moon, that is to say under an omen, but like all of them, neutral) in a private clinic, with my mother anaesthetized and surrounded by masculine midwives all graduated in obstetrics. The poor woman was forty-two years old and she was giving birth for practically the first time, for in the only preceding delivery she had produced a dead and diminutive monster. This nonexistent brother or sister was not spoken of in my house, and the only thing I knew was that it had the luck which Judas lacked: fortunately it had not been born alive, all for the better considering how horrible it looked. Although there are now those who say that inside I am a monster, on the outside, when I was born, I had an angelic aspect, and when my mother awoke from the anesthesia she gave thanks to heaven, to the obstetricians wearing splattered gowns and to my father who circumspectly studied the new scion, remembering the arduous moment of its conception.

It is dogma that there was a woman who, without knowing a man, found herself fertilized by the Infinite. I will not argue about it. Nor do I understand it. I have never known a virgin, nor am I interested in making the acquaintance of one. It has never seemed to me an indignity that my mother, upon delivering me and even before, was not a virgin, and I do not know why there could have been someone who would claim to have a mother who was a virgin or a virgin mother (*"inviolata, integra, et casta es, Mater purissima"*). Thus I allude to the amorous memory of my parent's embrace.

I will never reveal the dates of my conception and birth. I know how sincerely astrologers enjoy exercising their dimwitted rite, plotting coordinates and compasses which explain the hidden aspects of a temperament. There they are; I hope that they squander their intellects on their stale and simple conjectures about absurd intergalactic influences which the distant and proximate celestial bodies (those that are burning and those that have already burnt out) infuse in our dark destiny. They must know, whatever my complicated zodiac sign may be, with its ascendants and descendants, that I have been created completely impervious to superstition. To all superstition and to all omens for the same thing happens in this subject as in precipices: if you submit at all, you plunge headlong without any possibility of return. All we have to do is let ourselves believe in one superstition, even

in one of the most innocuous (black cats, the number thirteen) and we fall headlong without any possible return until
we find ourselves devoted assiduously to each one, to the
innumerable gods of Olympus.

I recount only the acts which molded, in my past, my
present: like my baptism, at the hands of the archbishop and
uncle, in the private chapel of the Palace, with such illustrious godfathers as the young philosopher Gonzalez and, not
yet matron but already chef, Sofia Ospina. It is not the celestial bodies which dictate a destiny for us. Neither is it the
fairy tale godmothers, nor the enchanted godfathers, although
from these I retain an antipathy for our typical regional dishes
(no less strong than that which I have for the foreign ones)
and a certain inclination to irreverent digressions.

The most accurate summary of a life is the precise re-
counting of the people that we have encountered during our
trajectory. It is not ourselves but others who determine the
sense our existence will have. I would not be who I am if I
had not encountered and lost Angela Pietragrua, my dark
priest uncles, the servant girls of my parents' house, my beloved Bonaventura (custodian of my secrets), and all of my
relatives and friends. Even one as reticent as I have always
been, is finally that which he is thanks to his contacts with
others.

At this stage I notice that, as always, I have forgotten to
talk about my friends. I have always claimed to be a much
better friend of Plato than of the truth, for on truth you
cannot rely (unfaithful and prostituting, slippery and vari-
able), while friends are unique. But I have not spoken of my
friends. My guide, my beloved Cunegunda, owner and lady of

mine, confirms this for me. Of all the many pages and pages I have dictated to her during these long weeks, I have said little or nothing to her of my friends. I have them on both sides of the ocean, of all sexes, of many ages, alive and dead. I exaggerate. Or I explain myself badly. When I say of all ages, I don't mean to say that today, now, here, I have fifteen-, twenty-five-, forty-, sixty- and eighty-nine-year-old friends. I mean to say that, fugitive creatures of the past, they were once those ages. I am, by now I have said it a thousand times, everything that I was. And I was a friend, for example, when I was fifteen and he was seventeen, of Manuel Saldarriaga.

Manuel was a somnambulist, a romantic poet, a lunatic, a wise man. Among the final images I have of him, I see myself at his side crouching on the roof tiles of his house watching dark swallows whirl up into the air. We are drinking a collection (stolen from the bar in his house) of little bottles of liquor: green mint liqueur, brown coffee liqueur, pale gin, urine-colored whiskey, faded red wine, muddy sugar-cane brandy and all the others. As we invent undrinkable cocktails, we discuss the surest methods for killing oneself. The revolver, the cliff, the feigned accident, the rope hanging from a beam, the poisons, rotgut, pills, the top floor of the Empire State Building, the center of the sea, the peak of Chimborazo. We didn't know anything about euthanasia or free death. We linked together ideas that would distract us from where we were. And we laughed ourselves to death at every solution. Tied to a mare's tail, underneath a truck on the freeway, bitten by a rattlesnake at the zoo, drowned and floating downstream, in a lukewarm bathtub. We didn't seem to be talking seriously, we were drunk and we were playing at being dead.

Saldarriaga was capable of writing two hundred and ten poems in a single night, and at least eight were good, which isn't bad. The whole neighborhood complained about the incessant tiptap of his nocturnal typewriter. After months and months of insistence on the keyboard they became accustomed to it, like one becomes accustomed to the tick of an alarm clock. We played chess and he nearly always beat me. We attended the same high school, but since he was older we were in different classes. The priests tormented him for he studied very little. We had a secret alphabet in which we wrote each other innocuous letters, but they prohibited us from using it in the school because the director of discipline was unable to decipher the code.

Manuel was tall, thin, awkward, with long, emaciated hands, like those painted by El Greco. He feasted on chocolates and his mouth was always blurred with brown due to the voracity with which he devoured them. We passionately read the modernist poets and Manuel, like them, dressed all in black from head to toe. In every verse of his there were shadows and words of Silva and even white waterlilies from Rubén Darío, heliotropes from Lugones and sighs from Barba Jacob. His last letter began with a verse from Gutiérrez Nájera that I no longer remember, but that had to do with death denied. We saw each other every day until I submerged myself in the kisses of Eva Serrano, and he in the distrustful embrace of one of the neighborhood girls. ˑ

One morning, at school, they called us to the chapel. To pray for the desperate intentions of a reckless colleague. It would not do any good, but at least the family would find some comfort in seeing the whole school down on its knees. Manuel, fed up with walking this earth, like the poets he imitated in his verses, had shot himself in the heart.

It was the first time that I felt sadness in all of its fullness. That sordid, dark and, arid weight which doesn't explode in tears but in a pensive pain, dry (thus it was described once, sorrowfully, by Quitapesares), without screams and without relief. Out of fidelity to the cry of a poet we had read only a few days before, I also did not want to see him. Neither on the floor of his bedroom where the opaque stain of his blood remained for years, nor in the stretcher upon which they removed him to perform the autopsy, nor in the clear and unvarnished wood coffin. Due to the intercession of my uncle the archbishop he was buried in sacred ground, but without a public mass, in accord with the merciless custom of those days. It did not matter if the suicide victim was seventeen or seventy, nor that the family desired a burial like that of any ordinary Christian. I don't know if I went to the cemetery, I don't remember, but I imagine that I did. Now when I think of him, almost sixty years later, I see him seated next to me, on the tile roof of his house, reciting both his own and other's verses or talking, as a way of killing time, about the best techniques for killing yourself.

Shortly after Manuel's suicide, I met Diego Velasquez. I'm not referring to the painter, but to a young man (without a mustache) who was called by the same name. I imagine that Socrates' least conscientious pupils and Catalus' most lubricious adolescents would have been like him. He was vital as a colt, luminous as a tube of neon, and silent as a broken hi-fi. These are my similes; I never was a good poet.

After Manuel's death I would have preferred gloomy friends, but it seems to me, although now I'm not sure, that the enemy of mine who bears my name tied the hands and feet of his companion who suffered with indignation his abandonment by Diego Velasquez.

There is a hidden place in the memory (I have so many memories that they don't fit in my head) where I know that digging violently I will discover the hand of Diego Velasquez (the right, the left?) shaking the hand of someone whom I called me. If I rummage further in the depths, I seem to remember the pebbles of a different waterfall than that beside which Eva Serrano had taught me the rituals of the tongue. I also seem to perceive the maritime undulation of a hammock, the buzz of eleven mosquitoes, and the hand of Diego Velasquez which, rather than caressing me, seems to draw my body. The hand of someone, who like me was called Gaspar Medina, also runs over Velasquez's body and suddenly that hand that was mine fills up with a viscous and hot liquid; Velasquez's hand also fills with semen and both of us anoint our bellies with the same ointment.

It's like a silent movie, in black and white, seen many years ago. And it's the muteness of the memory which indicates to me that Diego Velasquez did not even want to acknowledge the affair. That which is not spoken of, that which is not said, we can relegate to that dream territory of mute unreality. That disgusting one who was called by my name suffered his own silence, incapable of expressing himself, as well as the shameful silence of Diego Velasquez.

I see, like a lightning bolt, a train that travels full of noise and chickens towards Puerto Berrio; it's as hot as the bellows of hell, and the adolescent that I was is sitting on the roof of the train alongside Diego Velasquez. A tunnel darkens our view and cools the sweat which sticks to our shirts; in this parenthesis of twilight, Diego Velasquez's hand squeezes mine to announce that that night, beneath the rhythmic fluttering of the ventilators of Hotel Magdalena of Puerto Berrio, I will again feel my hand moistened by Velasquez's darkest current, his hand dampened by my symmetric and almost simultaneous eruption.

And now all of this converted into an antique silent film, prohibited for minors, and never projected to the public. The private virtue of an adventure so distant that it seems alien. The little that I can revive no longer moves my fibers. When I tried to repeat the handling with other hands and members, my will had vanished, the goat-like odor of male humans banished me from that entangled intercourse which was never considered base among the wisemen of antiquity. But that whom I called me, after the fondling under the ceiling fans of Puerto Berrio, suffered a desperate heartache when the namesake of the painter of *The Maids of Honor* pretended not to see me when looking at me, or preferred to look in another direction.

I remember a discussion in the classroom from around the same time. Since they had repeatedly caught the boarders masturbating together, the chaplain felt it was opportune to call them to order in public, reminding us how unnatural the affair was and directing us to note that animals never did such things. Had we perhaps ever seen a stallion mount another stallion? I see myself raising my hand and standing up to respond to him (I see the priest blushing with rage) that horses also do not speak, not because they are less natural, but because they have less fantasy. Very few activities would remain available for men if they limited themselves to imitating horses. And even beyond that, in imitating their sexual habits, we could end up mounting our own mothers. I see myself standing and that's how I note it in the corrected version of my life; it's a pity that the Gaspar Medina of those days was so naked of arguments, so innocent of the world that he had to leave his lips pressed together, accepting this obscene zoological misrepresentation. But at times, to aid this difficult affection which one feels for oneself, it is better not to remember ourselves as we were, but as we would like to have been.

Eighteen

Whose Theme is Skirt-Chasing,

Featuring Virgelina Pulgarin,

Alias the Proletarian.

I DON'T SMOKE EITHER TOBACCO OR ANYTHING ELSE, NOR HAVE I ever been a smoker. Not to protect my own health or the health of others, but because I don't like it. Nevertheless I cannot stand the salubrious customs of recent decades. In this northern part of the world, although truly the vice was imported from North America, they have given themselves over to persecuting those who damage others by smoking. Alarming figures of dangers to passive smokers are published and thus they exile the active ones, if they're lucky, to the attic. Passive smoke is harmful, yes, it's true—and living too is harmful, and laughter wrinkles the corners of the mouth and thinking fills the forehead with lines and food excavates the stomach. I don't smoke, but if I arrive at someone's house and that someone prohibits his guests from smoking, I get up, courteously shake hands, and leave. Or at least I write here that I leave, as truly I don't have the character, or I am too educated to behave in such a manner. Accomplices to this growing wave of prohibitions can go to hell.

Although I like vegetarians, I loathe (I always exaggerate with verbs) those who prohibit meat eating. I like the Quixote so much that I detest those who make it mandatory reading in high schools and universities. I love awakening in the early morning and I can't stand alarm clocks. I prefer ten masses to the third commandment. And I won't go on any more, because I also don't like preachers, not even those who advocate tolerance.

Permissiveness, lack of discipline, libertinism: phrases that have pursued me since childhood. My parents were always accused of pampering me, that is to say, of permissiveness, lack of discipline, and libertinism. I did more or less what I wanted. And they indulged me in almost everything, which is what you do to get a spoiled child. I could, for example, answer my parents. I never experienced those absurd scenes acted out in my friends' houses; the father demanding explanations: "Where is the ball? Why don't you pay attention to where you leave things?" The son silent, shaking in his boots. The father insists: "Where did you leave the ball? Answer me!" The son decides to answer: "Well, since it was mine, because they had given it to me, I..." And the father interrupts him furiously: "Don't talk back to me! Go to your room right now!" Or that other head of the family that, beside himself with rage, shouts at his happy son: "Ricardo, don't scream!" Thus is the authoritarian life of normal families, those who criticized my parents.

They expelled me from the Brelan Club, when all is said

and done, for not accepting prohibitions. Tacit prohibitions, on top of it all, which are the worst kind. And also because I believe in the rules, but I believe much more firmly in the exceptions. The first prohibition of a private club doesn't have anything to do with what one is, but with what one seems to be. There, basically, you can be whatever you want to be, a thief, a trafficker, a pimp or a criminal, as long as you don't seem like one.

It is a mental custom in Catholic countries. To seem libertine, in this environment, is much more serious than actually being libertine. Sin does not exist—or it has a more acceptable form of existence—so long as it is not revealed, or worse yet, vindicated. There is a rational motive for this: the person who exhibits or flaunts a sin, or at least doesn't cover it up, is in some way defending it, diffusing it. Concealing a sin is granting it a measure of censure, which is to say almost condemning it. I do something bad, but at least I hide it to indicate that I am ashamed of doing it.

Thus the efficiency of the sacrament of confession is not limited to the catharsis of vomiting all the evils committed. The inviolable secrecy of the confessional is as important as the catharsis, for it permits us to continue doing the same things without anybody finding out. And their infinite repetition permits us, more importantly, to repent the twisted path over and over again, without ever abandoning it. Nobody knows about it and the confessional pardons me; he who sins and prays comes out tied; everything, in the long run, and as long as it is done discreetly, is permitted or at least pardoned. You cannot survive in a Catholic country without respecting this rule, and even less in a private club in a Catholic country.

I had inherited membership in the Brelan Club from my parents. It is the most exclusive in the city, that one where important business deals were made, and where mayors, ministers and governors were elected. I learned to swim there, I learned to play tennis, golf and bridge there; it was there that I learned to drink whiskey, like a little English sprout transplanted to the tropics. I would go there with my school chums, and with the well-known rich boys from the university.

And it was there that I began to take a happy, impetuous, unruly young lass, who had the not so small defect of being (and seeming to be) poor and from the mountains: Virgelina Pulgarin Huitaca, alias the Proletarian. It was somewhere in the sixth decade of my years (and the seventies of the century), a few years after my political experience, which just maybe I'll recount next, and I was fed up with speeches and ethyl alcohol. The unerasable memory of Angela Pietragrua was fading, and to finally get her off my back I took refuge between the thighs and the tender crotch of that village adolescent, Virgelina, celebrating in the club, the temple of the wealthy doyens of my hometown.

There are, or there were, reserved rooms in the Brelan Club, for dark business. And a swimming pool that was vacant at certain hours. There was also a sauna, a Turkish bath, a gymnasium, and baths equipped with massaging jets of cold and hot water which we called Scottish but which are now called by a Japanese name. Sacred sites where the Proletarian and I sparked scandal. They gave the nickname to my Virgelina Pulgarin during a meeting of the Board of Directors when they were discussing the problem. The problem of member

Medina and, and... What could they call her if they didn't know her name? If her surname was not one of those like one's own?... the Proletarian! You could tell from a mile off that she was from a poor neighborhood and a humble family. I don't know how to describe the signs of this disparity of rank very well, but any member of the Brelan Club can recognize the stigma of poverty on the fly. It is denounced by a certain shade of the skin which is not easily disguised with make-up (for it is one thing to be of mixed descent, and another to look like you are), a certain manner of picking up a fork and raising a cup, a hidden crease in the clothing, an accentuated wear of the shoe's soles, and above all a certain manner of pronouncing words while asking for a simple rum and coke, a glass of water (she said "a glass *with* water"), or the check. I am not Pygmalion, and truly I liked the authentic guffaw and the open legs of the Proletarian, thus I never bothered myself with moderating the evidence of her provenance.

The guards and doormen of the grounds, in any case, were best at recognizing her stigma. Like those class-conscious guard dogs who can detect the approach of a beggar from a block away, in just the same way the doormen were the first who wanted to impede the entrance of my companion. I imposed her admission with bribes and an authoritarian voice. But then along came this other bone that was more difficult to gnaw on, the Administrator of the Brelan Club.

His name was Gilberto Loreto and he had family obligations. Had he not been a submissive and social climbing functionary, just his kinky hair and his vendor's voice would have impeded (no less than in the case of my lass) his crossing the racist threshold of the Brelan Club.

The Proletarian, since her childhood, had dreamed of getting acquainted with the inside of the recreational home of my town's wealthy, and I promised to present it to her, right down to its most hidden nook. I showed her the place and I showed myself off with her in the salons of every color (the Red, the Gold, the one with the ugly frescoes by Otoniel). She belched in the mirrored bar after having skimmed (that's how she said it) a whole bottle of beer in one gulp. She cleaned the nail of her little finger with the middle tine of a silver fork. To her the rocking chairs seemed old, the paintings dark, and the tables of the old colonial salon dusty. She called the waiters by waving her hand and yelling out to them, "What's up, brother?" She planted a kiss on the nape of my neck every two minutes and then she would send her hand to the market (these are her expressions) to see if my Don Giovanni was getting animated (I write this in my own more cultured slang). She greeted in the hallways, without knowing them of course, the founding members, and she said to me without lowering her voice, "What a cute cat, what a shame that he smells like pee." But more than anything else she said to Loreto, "You aren't so refined as all these others, why don't you come over and have a drink with me?"

Everything except this instinctive recognition of a member of the same class was acceptable to Administrator Loreto, who in the following meeting of the board of directors presented the problem of the honored member Medina (ex-candidate for the Senate) and his unrefined girlfriend, the Proletarian. I received a first, very discreet, letter, in which an article of the bylaws of the club was quoted to me. It stated that the members could invite persons to the campus, but that they were responsible for their acts and their behavior. The members, and even more especially their guests, must follow elementary rules of civility and decorum. They ended the letter politely. I, as if the affair had nothing to do with me, continued attending the club with my Virgelina Pulgarin.

I had fun with her. After the first few visits she navigated the club like Peter in his playhouse. I whispered in her ear the names of the members that she pointed out to me with her index finger, and without the mediation of any introduction she began to call them by their first names. To the president of the manufacturer's association, Echevarria Uribe, she would say, "What's new, Felix, lots of horses or what?"—and well I had told her that he played polo and I had explained that it was more or less soccer with bats and horses; she assaulted the owner of the Tupinamba chain of hotels, exclaiming, "You, Mauricio, don't have even one room available to sleep with me?"; Enrique Angel, owner of the largest local newspaper, she challenged, "Dear little Enrique, is it true that you're going to defend the Somozas?" And thus it continued until the second, more direct missive, arrived. Either my customary companion behave in a more respectful manner or an order would be imparted to the guards to impede her entrance, *ipso facto*.

I did not inform the Proletarian of these warnings; she noticed only that she was the center of attention when she entered one of the salons. For quiet a few afternoons I distracted her, trying to teach her the subtleties of bridge, until one day, bored with contracts and marks, she shouted at me,

"What a bunch of bullshit this game is! I like five-card stud better." She got up and went to the table where Doctor Mora White, ex-governor and rector of the Universidad Pontificia, was sitting. Pulling him by the sleeve she dragged him from the table where he was falling asleep in front of three other players, and forcibly led him to another salon to dance a *pasodoble*. Despite the fact that it had been years since Mora White had enjoyed such animated moments, the following day, at the front gate, I was received with a "Doctor Medina, please be kind enough to ask your friend to wait for you in the street."

Although I had foreseen what would happen, I had not prepared my reaction to the harsh events. Without thinking through what I would do, I asked the doorman to call Loreto, the Administrator. He made me wait a quarter of an hour. Finally he presented himself and in a syrupy voice, told me that it had nothing to do with him, that the decision had been imposed by "the Board," that his words in defense of the lady had been to no avail. I could not endure this spectacle of hypocrisy and as I could do nothing to revoke the decision of the Board, I began to insult him, to scream at him—ass-kisser, sell-out, sneak. Loreto for years had been cultivating a dark rancor for each and every one of the members of the club who, at the same time as they humiliated him day after day, gave him the salary to support his family. My public insults offered him the possibility of a singular, diminutive vengeance. Thus it was that the following day I received a letter of suspension for two months, due to my impertinent behavior with the administrator of the club, who had done no more than fulfill his duties.

The Proletarian, sitting to my right in the car, bent over her knees and cried throughout the whole ride home. Before the very humble doorway of the building where she lived I swore to her that I would never return to the Brelan Club until the order that impeded her from entering was revoked. And I kept my word, even after my geographic comings and goings led me to lose track of the Proletarian's steps.

Thinking of my vow, I set foot in the Brelan Club once again many years later, when I heard that Doctor Mora White, a widower of a few months, was celebrating his second matrimony. The gala party was celebrated in the Gold Room of the Brelan Club, and although they had not invited me I wanted to witness the triumphal entrance of Mrs. Virgelina White, previously the Proletarian, almost unrecognizable, who climbed the stairs of the club arm-in-arm with the ex-rector of the Pontificia. She threw me a glance over her shoulder, not because she had recognized me, but for exactly the opposite reason: she couldn't imagine who could be so lacking in manners as to arrive at her wedding without a tuxedo. It was evident that if Virgelina continued being a poor woman, by now she had learned to not seem like one. Gilberto Loreto recognized me. He was still administrator of the club but by now he was an actual member as well. From his narrow suit and with an amnesia that I believe was sincere, he asked me: "Doctor Medina, why haven't you been coming to the club?"

Nineteen

Wherein a Delightful Affection for
Cunegunda Bonaventura is Confessed.

OH, CUNEGUNDA, CUNEGUNDA, INNOCENT AND CHASTE AND
simple Cunegunda. How would you want me to introduce you to my friend Quitapesares, silent admirer of your
breasts? But my dearest one, anguish of my years, flower of
my decadence, bit of my broken heart (as a sad ballad would
say), haven't you understood any of what I have dictated to
you? Quitapesares, my beloved friend, who could he be but a
false boustrophedon, the most expensive mask, the disguise
for my readings. Oh, Cunegunda, understand, my Quitapesares'
are the books I read, the writings which give me strength to
survive the putrefaction of time which grows within me. Long
are the years and they are many now with me, with fresh
winds gone, gone, gone. Are these verses mine? Of course
not, my amiable Cunegunda, they are Quitapesares', that
demiurge of a thousand heads, one, plural and infinite.

Thought, in my case, is a mountain of superimposed phrases. Others people's phrases, clearly, one of my favorite sayings announces that all aphorisms are foreign. All of them, perhaps even this one that I dictate to you. But today I want to speak about you.

I am solitary with Cunegunda Bonaventura, and only in her company do I feel perfect solitude. I have reached the extreme of only being able to be alone when she is with me. I am not referring to the absurd tranquility of never glancing at her, without remorse, or the base serenity of being able to scratch my armpits without hiding the gesture: it is also a mental solitude, of thought which flows without having to make any concession to the other. She never asks me to explain anything if I talk; she doesn't ask me to speak, or to be quiet, and never would she interrogate my silence. I don't know if she understands my silence or my words (I think not, many times) but she assents, consciously, she listens, she is quiet. She also protests, denies, screams, shouts, but since she is a specialist in dissent, in criticizing what I do or what I write (she is not often mistaken), when I become infuriated with her observations, she retires, and waits until it passes: she knows that he who is most capable of waiting is the true victor.

If I am sad she doesn't complain, if I am happy she doesn't celebrate. It is like living with a dog, says my friend Quitapesares, who is a simple simplifier.

Solitude is living with Cunegunda. There exists no test or criteria for evaluating her intelligence. She is brilliant and foolish at the same time, at once holy and malignant, good and evil, calculating and naïve. When I rest my face upon

Cunegunda's chest, I am almost always surprised to find that something palpitates there within. She walks silently through the library, barefoot, and she seems to be floating a few inches above the floor. If I believed in levitation I would say that I have seen her levitate. And I haven't seen it, but her body has a mystical lightness.

She is flesh and blood, Cunegunda, and well, every time this tremendous doubt (that of whether she is simply a spiritual being) has assaulted my judgment, I have grabbed the whip to flog her. I use a spelling error as a pretext and I beat her until blood sprouts from her back. Afterwards I lean over her and lick her wounds and salt them with my tears. Cunegunda smiles like a saint before his hair shirt and she also kisses the hands that whipped her.

I met Cunegunda, like everything important that has happened in my life, by mistake. Neither she nor I knew that we were looking for one another: she a job, and I a secretary. We were both strolling in the Valentino Gardens, in this city of my likely entombment, I behind my cane, and she behind her boyfriend. Cunegunda was crying, and the boyfriend quickened his pace. I wanted to detain this injustice, I told her that it should not be this way, not like that. She told me the story, truly the only story of Cunegunda's that I really know, because she is a quiet woman. Maybe she will tell it one day, after my death, she herself, when she is rested from this dictation and has plenty of time. It is not a story that I should tell, but it is the story that bound us together that afternoon and now I think that there will not be enough time for it not to unite us forever.

Such are stories, an alliance between those who tell them and those who listen to them.

Twenty

A Jaunt Which Talks (Badly, Of Course) About a City & a Few of Its Houses.

MY CHILDHOOD IS COMPOSED OF MEMORIES OF A HOUSE OVER-flowing with women and doors. My mother and Tata; my mother, Tata and the caretaking nun, Sister Annunciation; my mother, Tata, Sister Annunciation and the cook; my mother, Tata, Sister Annunciation, the cook and Benilda and Manuelita and Tomasa, the three indoor girls; my mother, Tata, Sister Annunciation, the cook, Benilda, Manuelita, Tomasa, and Adela the ironer; my mother, Tata, Sister Annunciation, the cook, Tomasa, Benilda, and Manuelita, Adela the ironer, and the extended visits of aunts (Maruja, Julia, et cetera).

Not to speak of the doors: the front door, the back door, the door to the yard, the door to the library, to the master bedroom, to the guest room, to the laundry room, to the pantry, to the maid's room, to my room, to the rooms of my little brothers who never arrived, to the sewing room, to the game room, to the immersion bathroom, to the other bathrooms, and to the chapel which was never opened again after the death of my uncle the archbishop. The women moved like ants from early in the morning, and I remember that the first thing they did was sweep the ceilings with long-handled brooms (my mother was terrified by one of my father's tremendous prophecies: "This house will be ruined the day that there are four spiderwebs in each of the four corners of a room's ceiling."). Never, as long as they were alive, were there spiderwebs in the corners of the ceilings of my house.

I had not thought about that until today and I get up to inspect the corners of the ceiling of my house in Turin: in three corners there are blackened tatters of webs abandoned by their owners. I call Rosario the cook and I order her to tell the fruit of her womb, Jesus, that he resolve this problem by tomorrow, for the house that they will inherit is about to fall into ruin. This last sentence seems exaggerated to her, but she assents.

My house, a large mansion in El Poblado, was knocked down to construct an apartment building for *haute bourgeois* and recently elevated *mafiosi*. But I do not complain, for the error was mine. One fateful day of weak character, almost ten years ago, I signed the authorization which the administrator had requested to sell it; he said that it was the perfect moment, for in just a few years, El Poblado, which was becoming overcrowded, would begin to decline in value. As a city planner he was correct: the neighborhoods of the rich do not stay put, they continually move farther and farther away. Away from the *nouveau riche*, from the half-rich and from the poor, who all of the others attract. You have to dangle off hills (higher, ever higher) or change floors, move to Rionegro, to Llanogrande, which is where I go now when I return to my country. I arrive at what was one of my parents' country houses, the cool high-country estate, charged with childhood memories for we used to go there to "be temperate" during December vacations. The weekend country house, where Eva Serrano gave me those memorable kisses, was a little closer, in Sabaneta. My childhood is constructed of memories of these estates: the one in Cauca, the one in Amalfi, the one in Sabaneta. The one in Rionegro was the oldest and had the advantage of being in the location where one could most approximate the cold Decembers of the motherland, with a lit fireplace and imitation snow made from cotton—for a warm Christmas was inconceivable. It was like the house in Sabaneta with pastures and stables. A typical Spanish colonial house with a courtyard in the center and a well in the middle of the courtyard. All of the bedrooms opened on to that square courtyard. Or do open, I should say, for despite the insistence of the administrator, I have not wanted to sell or demolish the house. It is very close to the rabble, now, and to a jail, but what can you do.

The Rionegro house is the one I like best. The town, in its growth, has come threateningly close. The leftist mayors have wanted to appropriate my best pastures to construct public housing, those little crowded-together houses where they cram three couples, each of them with eight children. They reproduce like rabbits, my dear countrymen, and they no longer fit in the town. I don't want to give up the pastures where the great-great-granddaughters of the cows I knew in

my youth are still grazing. The dairy loses money and the
administrator sends me one fax after another telling me that
the business is not profitable. I should sell the cattle, there is
a Liberal mayor now and he would buy the land from me for
more than it's worth, I should take advantage of the situation, I can't keep running the risk that the rabble might
invade our pastures. I always answer with the same words.
Actually I have saved the paper, written in my own hand,
which says: THE RIONEGRO ESTATE IS NOT TO BE
TOUCHED! And each time that he proposes selling, I send
him a fax of the same page. It seems that he doesn't understand, although he does it for my own good.

The entrance to the Coquette—that's the name of the
Rionegro estate—is off of the old highway to Santa Helena,
just before you enter town. It is surrounded by an eight-foot-
high white adobe wall, crowned with ceramic tiles, that my
great-grandfather had his Negroes make just before slavery
was abolished. It's a beautiful adobe wall, for those who say
that nothing survived from those barbarous times: now the
slaves are paid and they live in worse conditions and do less.
Furthermore, they are convinced that they are no longer slaves,
and yet they still are. The gateway is a taller adobe structure,
with an arch, and steel bars in the Andalusian style. A narrow lane bordered by Brazilian araucaria trees leads through
the garden to the house. Upon arriving one is greeted by the
barking of the grandchildren of the German shepherds I
brought to Colombia thirty years ago. The house has an antique terra-cotta floor, and portraits of my ancestors since the
conquest, although, to be honest, the supposed ancestors from
the sixteenth and seventeenth centuries are completely false

and their faces were invented based on their descendants (almost all of them look a great deal like my great-grandfather).

Now, in addition, they have set the new airport very close by, and the atrocious airplanes of Avianca pass by grazing the leaves of my araucarias. Or almost. Ah, how I used to enjoy the arrival at the old airport. It was a testimony, a perfect parable of the culture of my town. Nothing made me laugh more than landing in that grotto. Because of that, and only due to that, I refused to sign the petition to convert the old airport into a park. It should remain as it was, a living monument to our stupidity, to our lack of taste, to our impossible vulgarity. There we have three delights united: the noisy airport, the silent cemetery, and the exclusive golf course of a private club. Landing in my city (once in jets, now in helicopters) is the perfect demonstration that the other parts of the world are, more or less, purgatory, but this place in which I had the amusing bad luck to be born and pass that time of life which seems eternal, youth—this revolting hole—is the unarguable confirmation that hell exists. Here, and not in the beyond.

Maybe on first glance you don't notice, if you are a foreigner and arrive on a clear day late in December, when the drought that they call summer is just beginning and it allows you to see a discreetly blue sky; when the rich of the town have gone off to temper themselves, on their holidays. You land and at the end of the runway, you see a Christ as big as the airplane, who opens his arms like wings before a nonexistent cross. The image of our Lord has recently been improved with a chaste patch or a loincloth which hides his

private parts. But do not believe that the decision is completely due to the timidity of the fateful cardinal, the future
John Jairo the First; according to what they say, no, his eminence had his good reasons for ordering the mantle. It happens that during landings a good part of the retinue (relatives
or their companions) fell into ecstasy in admiration of that
divine member with its asymmetrical celestial balls. Eager
bachelorettes, fat old men, nostalgic widows, imperfectly married discontents, declared faggots and ashamed pansies, adolescents with pimples, and girls in sandals, that is to say three-
quarters of the local population elevated their gaze towards
the middle of the holy body and sighed. Not one of them
noted the only remarkable aspect of Christ's genitals, that is
the historical (and evangelical) incompetence of the sculptor
who forgot to suppress the foreskin of the most famous Jew of
all time.

The airplane would land, and at the end of the runway
the passengers could appreciate God crucified in the air at
the gate to the largest cemetery in the city. This is the wel-
come they give tourists in hell: the most violent city in the
world receives its visitors with the apocalyptic vision of an
infinity of tombs. Threat, admonition, forewarning? It could
be, but I tend to think that it is pure and simple bad taste: in
relation to the travelers that they encounter as their wel-
come death in the image of whitened sepulchers, and in relation to the dead that, even if they are deaf as stones, must be
irritated by that vibration of dust and creaking of bones and
colliding of teeth that the bellow of the turbines provokes.

I attended the funeral of Juan Jacobo Rodo there, that
friend whom they killed for being a Communist. His com-

panions had to interrupt the speeches and rebellious declara-
tions twice due to a take off and a landing. And when they
had already foisted the coffin into its definitive pit, we saw a
rapid white volatile object falling from the sky that was not
the Holy Spirit, but the golf ball of an elegant adolescent
who was training in the neighboring club. The ball struck
the box with the report of a bullet, and the Communists, not
without a certain justification, took advantage of the moment to intensify even more their disjointed programs of vengeance against the oppressors.

The inferno of my country is at times fertile with surprises. The last time that I touched down, one Sunday, in
that airport golf course cemetery, I noted that the last of the
spaces was filled with people. The helicopter pilot explained
to me that the poor, noting that there was not one park for
them in the city, now made their weekend outings (which
the refined call picnics) in the cemetery. On top of the slab
went a clean tablecloth with pieces of chicken and fresh or-
anges on it. My friend Juan Jacobo Rodo, before they killed
him, assured me that one day—he was an optimistic sort—
the people of my valley would have a vast park, and they
would not only make their outings in the old cemetery, but
they would plant the legs of their grills in the holes of what
had been the golf course and they would roller-skate across
the breadth of the old runways of the air field. It will be in
the year two thousand eight hundred and eleven, I answered,
but he, optimistic in his sincere leaflet language, declared
that it was never too late for the rescue of the people.

In any case, my city has the dubious merit of being a
place that one never misses. It is a location that allows a

perfect uprooting, a city that, being one's own, can be viewed with indifference, with the neutrality of a tourist who doesn't encounter anything worth remembering. I didn't suffer from homesickness. Although I don't know. My friend Quitapesares asserts that my obsessive denial of nostalgia only reveals that I continue to be lost in it.

Twenty-One

In Which Something is Briefly

Remembered Which We Would Have

Preferred to Have Forgotten.

N O. THESE PASSAGES WHICH CUNEGUNDA IS READING TO ME are too miserable. I should erase myself, disappear. Or at least not recount those years during which I lost myself. Stripped of a future, for me the future had been filled only with the illusion of living with Angela Pietragrua, my life after her death was another death. I carried the worst facets of my personality to the extreme. Trying not to be me, but to be another. Trying to be a much worse person, much worse than myself. For example: in the mornings I would scatter talcum powder over my shoulders. On top of the dark jacket a dash of powder, on the shoulders, under the nape of my neck, with the only goal being creating the illusion of dandruff. Yes, I did not suffer from being scurfy, but I wanted to win a smile, a gesture of repugnance in the glances of passersby. They should believe I had dandruff.

I have said that eating does not excite me. Well, I fattened myself up like a pig. I bought the leftovers in the butcher's shop, fatty meat, grease, suet, lard, giblets. And fighting back a desire to vomit I consumed it all. I gained fifty pounds in six months, the rolls of my belly folded over my belt, my face swelled up, I didn't recognize myself in the mirror, others didn't recognize me on the street. I wanted to be ugly and I achieved it. I was never able to fully recover.

I bought my street clothes in the Balon, Turin's flea market. Out-of-date styles, frayed, and dark to augment the contrast of the little snowflakes of fictional dandruff. Third-hand shoes, jackets with a cut from the beginning of the century, shirts with their collars blackened by time, bowler hats worn smooth. Rumpled suits that I would wear without changing for at least two weeks.

I stopped bathing, I stopped brushing my teeth. I almost came to like the fetid fumes that rose from my armpits. I let my fingernails and toenails grow. And I didn't clean them, but left them filled with a disgusting black crescent.

I spoke in the impoverished style which I had always hated. I didn't use the real names of things—I called them all "shit." I didn't call feelings by their names, I called them shit. To explain why I didn't shave, I said: "You know if I use that shit, it's so shitty." I banished from my speech the joy of precision, I spoke like everyone else, and the worst part was that everyone understood me. I also embellished my speech with other swear words, I intercalated them in my insipid discourse: "'Cause well the bitch of it is, motherfucker, you know like, ah son of a bitch, you have shit that, I'm not fucking with you, is really fucking shit." I spoke like that.

I stored my furniture in a warehouse. I took down the
Picasso paintings and hung posters of Picasso paintings. I
bought modern furniture, I installed neon tubes to illuminate
the rooms of the house. I had the walls papered with Swiss
landscapes of snowy mountains and autumn hills. On top of
the wooden floor I had brown wall-to-wall carpeting installed.
I acquired plastic flowers in plastic vases. I bought perfumed
air fresheners to scent the environment. I bought Clayderman
records to create a sonorous ambiance for guests.

I sucked my fingers and picked my nose before my guests.
In the very same way I scratched my balls, stuffing my hand
down into my pants. I scratched my head without bothering
to disguise it—well, of course it itched since I never bothered
to wash my hair; greasy, it was crawling with parasites. Thus
I lived various years. That was the mourning that I was obliged
to endure for the death of my beloved Angela Pietragrua,
dead in delivery due to the labors of the infectious semen of
the Viscount of Alfaguara.

That's all I will now recount.

When this terrible period of prostration ended, this deliberate deformation of my body and my habits, I wanted to
return to being me. But before I could, for a time, I had to
stop being anybody. I had been me, I had converted myself
into an anti-me; to again be myself I had to be nobody for a
time. I think I was starting the fifth decade of my existence
when I went to travel in mongrel territories, in countries that
were hidden and anonymous.

I had my hair cut so that it stood just an eighth of an
inch out from the leather of my cranium. I started wearing
big square glasses with tortoiseshell frames, and I grew a big

Mexican-style mustache. I resolved to wear a uniform, to use one set outfit: dark blue pants, a belt, low black boots, and shirts with sky blue stripes. I got rid of the clothes from the Balon as well as my old clothes: I gave away my suits and ties. I did not use my real name again.

I wanted to erase myself. Dissolve into the indistinct masses. No one would notice the perfect Sir Nobody. I made pilgrimages to remote locations around the world. With the rush of neither a tourist, nor of a devotee, I traveled without looking at anything. So as to have a goal, I followed the route of the earth's famous sanctuaries: I went to visit the Virgin of Guadeloupe, I sprinkled myself with the water of Lourdes, I was in Mecca, in the Holy Land, in Santiago de Compostela, in Tibet. I journeyed the great rivers, the Ganges, the Atrato, the Orinoco, the Mississippi, the Putumayo, the Amazon, the Danube, the Nile, the Volga, and many others. I didn't climb a single mountain, but I spoke with devotees of all of the religions, in Rome and in Calcutta and in Teheran; in Los Angeles, in Peking, and in Wittenberg.

Bit by bit I could return to being the shadow of Gaspar Medina. Yes, a man who doesn't feel. I found my refuge in total indifference. This I was able to achieve, converting myself into someone who is nothing, into someone who doesn't feel. But who nonetheless seemed like and would continue to seem like that one who had been called by my name. I grew out of my love for Angela Pietragrua just as the survivors exited the Lager. Many years passed before I was again able to begin to build (that is if you can call this flimsy frame a construction) on top of the ruins of that tremendous recollection.

Twenty-Two

A Memory in Which a Few Years Are Thrown Overboard.

IF ONLY THIS ALREADY TOO LONG HISTORY HAD A REASON, A line, a precise direction, instead of being an absurd zigzag. The memories have not grown like a line, in order, but instead through agglomeration like a raspberry. Or even better: like a cancer. The metastasis of my old age has propagated throughout the entire book, contaminating with my evil tongue even the luminous days of my less bitter youth.

I was a man ruined by the love of one single woman, Angela Pietragrua. There is little that I can say about my life after she disappeared. Nothing. A state of inactivity in this house or in the summer refuge in Pulignano, the only place, the only thing in the world which I continued enjoying. Journeys to the dark place where I was born, in which at each return I encountered more poverty, more putrefaction, more death. Before this depressing spectacle, for an instant, I had the dream of being a benevolent despot. For I did not see any other solution (nor do I now) for that nest of serpents. My incursion into active politics, when I was, or was almost, fifty years old, was a perfect failure.

I allied myself with chiefs of the worst character, with officers resentful of having been forced out of the service early, with unruly students, with simpletons, nuisances, lapdogs, sneaks, sycophants. Stupid people in whom I invested millions for nothing. My tyranny never grew beyond being a preposterous project, a mass delirium of drunks.

I discovered, in my old age, this secretary, my secretary, and the joy of remembering. Before an inexorably exhausted future, I opted to take refuge in that comfortable time of the already experienced. And Cunegunda taught me how to remember. It's not worth it to remember everything. These empty years after Pietragrua's farewell and before the encounter with Bonaventura don't deserve even the outline of a page. I rightfully forget them, in good taste and without regrets. There are years, situations, epochs, which deserve only our silence.

Why do you complain, curious Cunegunda? Can I not suppress the years of my life which I most hate? Maybe you are entertained by my alcoholic reflections on the games of Colombian politics? If you give me a taste of your fresh saliva, a wet kiss, a few drops of salty tears to liven up my cerebrum, if you ask me again, I will dictate to you my adventures as a politician among the cities and towns of my fatherland. Yes, I'll do it, even if it's only to wrap in the costume of a clown this hateful being who I obstinately persist in calling "me" (Quitapesares' words).

Twenty-Three

On the Drunken Relationship which Don Gaspar Medina Had with Politics, In Addition to a Pleasant Monastic Experience.

THAT FIFTY-YEAR-OLD EXPATRIATE, SUDDENLY INSTALLED IN A mansion in the rainy capital of the country where he was born; that voluntary exile, that fugitive returned to the pig-sty of his native land; that mature man suffering from immaturity, who began to go bald, still doubled over by the pain of fifteen years of exhaustive remembering of the woman he briefly loved; that Gaspar Medina (Urdaneta according to baptismal burdens), with dictatorial intentions (or desires of a benevolent despot), with nostalgia for a restoration and more than anything suffering from the tedium of life, raided politics.

The National Front, that infamous accord mandating that each of the two major political parties take turns in the presidency, came to an end, and he began—or I began—by scheduling a meeting with the most illustrious of the local political leaders. After half an hour of vapid discussion the Honorable Senator Ecks, an impressive speaker, was drunk. His lackey, a representative to the Chamber, was drunk. The Minister of Education was drunk. His mistress, who was vice minister of the same department, was drunk. The President of the Second Commission of the Senate was drunk. The bold leftist councilor was drunk. The Coronel (retired) Armando Armando was drunk. Could there be any politician, in any corner of my country who wasn't drunk? I don't think so. In those days, and who knows until when, the politicians of my nation were either drunk, or they were on their way to getting drunk, or they were sleeping drunk, or in the last possible scenario they were suffering from a hangover.

I, Gaspar Medina, sober, despite everything continued speaking for months of my project to make the country a less savage territory. A proposal which as a project didn't even have a name; in reality I harangued them with phrases taken from Laureano, from Gaitán, from López Pumarejo, from Santander, from Bolívar, from Martí. I made my speeches like puzzles, like a collage, inserting the phrases of one or another, one after another, to please all of the tendencies. I also translated from the Italian fragments of Mussolini and Togliatti; from the Argentine cries of Peron, from the Guarani, outbursts of my Paraguayan namesake, Gaspar de Francia, and I mixed them into this soup of letters with neither head nor tail. But, honestly, nobody listened to me; they were all drunk.

They paid homage to me in the clubs. They charged I-don't-know-how-many dollars per head, all of which ended up in the pockets of the hosts, for they passed me the bill for the whiskey, the rental of the hall, the waiters, the flowers, the appetizers and the food, in short, for everything. Senator Ecks, my leading sponsor, from his frog face, bloated and red

from dozens of brandies, spit out the discourse which introduced me as the new savior of the fatherland. "Beeecauause
Doctoor Gaspaar UUUrdaneetaa is a Dreeeameeer, iiis aaa
Dooon Quiiiixooooteeeee!" And I, wanting to resemble his
description, recounted the novel of the Curious Impertinent
or the Adventure of Braying, with very little success, of course,
among the crowd of illiterate drunks who called for more
whiskey, more rum, another brandy.

Until one day my tongue became weak: "Honorable ministers and senators, honorable representatives, good councilors,
deputies, governors and mayors, this country is being managed
by a pack of drunks: all of you!" There was a moment of silence,
but immediately all of the drunks applauded. What should I do?
In vain I consulted Vladimir Ilych, as I had been advised by the
drunken students of the National University: I fell asleep in the
third paragraph. Machiavelli, Montesquieu, Weber, I consulted
all of them in vain. The public was immune to words: regardless
of what I said, if I gave out enough liquor, they acclaimed my
speeches. I went along very well in politics.

Senator Ecks looked at me with his frog face, bloated. He
couldn't understand what I was trying to do by distributing so
much whiskey. I had been following the same plan for months,
not only without saving a single cent, but without, on top of
everything, aspiring to a specific post, or asking for a specific
favor, without proposing any racket. And I couldn't explain to
him that I was only trying to flee my memories (that is to say
that swamp in which Pietragrua had left me submerged), by
plunging into the mud of politics, although in reality politics
bored me more than reading a regional Serbo-Croatian novel.
Senator Ecks, half drunk, bloated, stared fixedly at me with his

frog face: "Doctor Urdaneta, what is it that you want?"

I proposed in my speeches, because I was bored and to see what would happen, initiatives that occurred to me from reading Swift: the prohibition of whiskey imports, or of radio transmission of football games, or of the public circulation of pregnant women, or of the production of rum in the coastal region, of brandy in the highlands and of the sale of beer in all of the river ports. If I had given out enough liquor, they cheered me. I proposed sterilizing all poor girls: they acclaimed me, drunk. Giving a vasectomy to all of the presidential candidates and perpetually exiling the sons of ex-presidents: they cheered me, all of them intoxicated: even the sons and grandsons of the ex-presidents. I sustained that it would be necessary to castrate rapists, amputate the hands of thieves, cut out the tongues of slanderers, tear out the right eyes of the overcurious: I received intoxicating ovations. Re-establish slavery, abolish the death penalty (that was already abolished for decades), make matrimony obligatory by twenty-eight for men and by twenty-two for women: I heard vivas and vivas, with a vivid alcoholic stench.

One day, during a reception with landowners I proposed a life sentence for guerrillas, the next day, in a working class neighborhood, the opening of the jails and the liberation of all political prisoners: volleys of applause from all sides. One day abolish the concordat with Rome, the next day, give a Volkswagen to every Catholic priest; hallelujahs from all sides. If I distributed whiskey, it was impossible for me not to be successful regardless of what it was I said, barbarous or sensible, straight or sinister, turbid or clear.

It was not hard to imagine how one could climb to power in a land of drunks. With votes? Bah, in this country power is bought with quarts of brandy in the mountain villages, with carafes of rum on the coast and with bottles of whiskey in the clubs of the people of my class. I became friends with the presidents of all of the liquor companies, with the tax inspectors, with the moonshine producers, with the beer brewers and distributors, with the whiskey importers. To manage this country (I discovered the strategy) one needed to control the sources of its poison, its alcohol factories.

That campaign slowly became, speech after speech, a collective delirium tremens. Columnists drunk as hounds, alcoholic reporters, commentators riding out their hangovers, all spoke well of this political phenomenon who had returned from Italy with the vigor of the best Roman orators. *Cicero of the Andes*, they called me, that tipsy bunch who changed from lethargic to euphoric with the little liquid that I gave out. From town to town a retching hiccuping crowd followed me; from town to town my caravan transported posters and bottles.

And all these towns, wrapped in the same alcoholic vapor, seemed the same to me—except for one, that of my ancestors the Urdanetas. My stay in that lofty population in the Andes, cradle of my great grandparents, whose name I would rather not mention here, was very pleasant. During the intoxicating electoral campaign it was necessary that we pass an afternoon in that little town to try and convince three or four thousand souls to vote for me.

The town I'm not mentioning, with six thousand voters, voted roughly ninety-six percent for the Conservative Party, bloody glory of my ancestors. The problem was that I had allied myself, as an electoral stratagem, with liberal senators. I had to, then, extend my stay there for a longer period, you

will see why, but with the pretext of convincing my countrymen to spontaneously change political parties.

The obvious way to achieve this was to put myself in contact with the local religious authorities—the clergy—traditional
allies of the conservatives. The first thing that I did was to stay
at the convent of the Mothers of Marie Poussepin, where the
local chaplain and the boss of the local clergy dwelled. I spoke
with the Reverend Mother Superior, I expressed my desire to
foster, from that instant, the education of country girls, and I
wrote a substantial check for the foundation which financed
the boarding of young girls. I signed it with pleasure, for throughout the campaign my checks had unfailingly come to rest in
liquor stores, breweries or whiskey importers.

Ah, how I remember the Reverend Mother Superior. From
our first glance, we got along well; she took one of my hands,
cold, between her lukewarm hands (without being able to
repress that tender common saying of "cold hands, warm
heart") and for a long moment we looked into each other's
eyes. "Doctor Medina, you will go far, you will do great things
for the land of your great-grandparents," she said to me while
I agreed without smiling.

The Reverend Mother Superior charged two sisters with
my care and service. They were two identical twins, Sister Maria
and Sister Maria (their middle names, alas, I could never remember) that had very recently arrived from their novitiate.
Young and sweet, with those glowing faces and that impeccable
complexion that actresses dream of, and only nuns attain. It was
impossible to distinguish them, recognize who was which, and
since one of the two of them was always with me, for they didn't
abandon me, I chose to call them both Sister Maria. I carry a

beautiful memory of those pious twins—a chaste and holy memory, suspicious reader and evil-thinking Cunegunda.

The Reverend Father Chaplain loaned me his private bedroom in the convent. It was fairly large (although, with his generous humility he called it a cell), full of angles and narrow nooks, and it was situated on the floor immediately above that of the boarder's bedrooms. I remember that in those days there were only fifty-three girls residing at the school. It was a joy to attend the daily mass, at five-thirty in the morning, and see those fifty-three country maidens file in. They had moved to the town from the nearby valleys, and they entered silently, freshly washed, hair carefully combed, fervent, almost moved to tears by the sacred ambiance of the chapel.

Their dark blue uniforms, quite long, their white blouses buttoned up to the collar, their hair still humid from the icy baths they were obliged to take before entering the chapel, their prolonged and inaudible confessions before the grill of the Chaplain's confessional... After the Eucharist we moved together to the Refectory where they treated us to magnificent country breakfasts (which disgracefully my palate was unable to appreciate) and at the table of honor, beside Sister Maria and Sister Maria, next to the Chaplain and beside the Reverend Mother Superior, each day ten different students ate their breakfast, selected according to their good behavior the previous day.

My visit to that town, thanks to my stay in that sedate and silent convent, was an unforgettable experience. The Chaplain didn't delay in showing his inclination to support my candidacy, and from that day on, he likewise didn't stop consuming the best bottles of different alcohols (although in the end they are all the same) that I had brought to the village. The very same

Mother Superior, upon assuring me that her vote and those of the rest of the sisters in the convent would be for me, got out a half dozen goblets and, with the two Marias and a few other nuns, toasted my health with a certain sanctifying wine which I had consigned to her upon my arrival.

After the speeches and the libations with the local leaders and the notable citizens, I retired with the Chaplain to his chambers on the second floor. There I assured him several times that if I was strategically united with the annoying liberals, it was because I had a secret purpose: to restore that ancient alliance between earthly and heavenly powers which had brought so many benefits to our beaten-down nation during past centuries. I remember that one night we toasted that restoration until the early morning: we opened more than three bottles of a stupendous sherry that I myself had taken charge of procuring in Andaluz territory.

I won't forget that daybreak when the chaplain, maybe a little exalted by the sherries, led me to a secret nook in his chambers, opened a little window, camouflaged in the floor under a Persian carpet, and allowed me to take in one of the most marvelous spectacles that my eyes remember. It was a quarter to five in the morning and the sun was beginning to stir behind the peaks of the Andes. The resident students, one by one, drowsy and slow, passed before our eyes, under our eyes, and they stripped off the long white nightgowns in which they slept. Shivering due to the chilly air off the peaks of the Andes, their tender little adolescent bodies seemed to gain more vigor, more vibration, more form. There were five, only five contiguous showers without divisions, for all of the residents, and I saw paraded before me all of the forms in which nature creates delicious juvenile bodies.

They were country girls of various ages, between thirteen and seventeen, of all colors, of all bearings and measurements. It was a delight to appreciate the marvelous ethnic chaos that the stupendous mixture of peoples of my fatherland has provoked, and to verify as well the psychological diversity of those virgins whose nipples flowered upon contact with the cold water. There were those who barely grazed their skin with soap and hands, and those who were voluptuous to the point of spasms during that sole moment in which they were permitted to caress their bodies. There were those of abundant flesh, of swollen breast and magnificent hips, and there those who were fine and delicate like ghostly apparitions.

I was going to express my admiration to the Reverend Father Chaplain, owner of that magnificent visual harem, but before I could open my mouth (or close it to speak, for it had already fallen open) I saw that he was spouting tears of happiness as he said to me: "Occasionally the Lord favors us with some small anticipation of paradise." And then I didn't say anything, for his words seemed to me to be more exact than any I could have uttered.

Even though I would have wanted to remain forever in that preview of the kingdom of heaven, I could not tarry too much longer. The Liberal politicians, drunken and bored in my absence, called me to order. They couldn't understand why the eight hours scheduled for the town had prolonged themselves into eight days. But it wasn't their twangy voices that pressed me to leave the town. What convinced me to speed up my departure was that I found out that the Reverend Mother, with the help of a few distinguished matrons, was determined to erect my statue in the town's central plaza. The affair of the statue wouldn't be so horrible; the bad part was that the Mother sustained that it would not be suitable for my presence to compare unfavorably with the nude Bolivar of the plaza, so that, it was necessary that a monument of me be made in just the same condition, equestrian and stark naked.

I had to abandon that harem for the eyes, much to my regret, for I saw myself posing in the middle of a stable, astride a stud rocinante, letting some incompetent sculptor take the measurements of my calves. And I should have stayed, despite it all, for from then on, during the whole political campaign, I didn't see anything worth a damn. I didn't see anything but drunks and more drunks.

For that very reason, when only a little time remained before the elections (and here I end this story which is intoxicating you, Cunegunda), and when my seat in the Senate was already assured, I resolved to leave all of that revel of drunks hanging on the pencils and stuck to the mouths of their bottles. I passed the reins of the movement to the Coronel (retired) Armando Armando, for I understood without shock, but with displeasure, that everyone, everyone in my country, the politicians who give the orders and the rabble who are ordered, the Maoist and Castroist guerrillas and smugglers, the leather, cloth and lily producers, the coffee, marijuana and poppy cultivators, the soldiers and the priests, the movie and theater actors, the poets and the novelists, the bolero, tango and vallenato singers, the cattlemen, the locksmiths, the violinists and the butchers, all of them, all of the voters, aspired to only one thing and continue to aspire to only one thing: to be good and drunk, definitively and forever dru-unk.

Twenty-Four

Wherein a Eulogy of Silence is
Proclaimed & What is Not Disclosed
in Passing Over Several Years of Life
is Declared.

Twenty-Five

*Gray Monologue with Which
the Quite Noble Don Gaspar Medina
Succeeds in Terminating His Memoirs.*

I T WOULD BE RIDICULOUS TO ASK YOURSELF HOW THIS STORY
will end; all stories terminate in the same way, every account follows the same path, whether evident or veiled. Interrupting them earlier is a whiny strategy for readers in search
of evasion and consolation. They married, they had children,
they lived happily ever after, they ate many chickens. Yes,
but they also died. All stories, according to Quitapesares,
lead towards death. Including Lazarus's tale. Why doesn't the
scripture recount that day upon which Lazarus, after having
been resuscitated, definitively died? I will; I have recounted
my resurrection, which is what I have written, and I will
recount my death.

One August Sunday in the desert of my vacant house.
Cunegunda has gone to the mountains or the city or the
ocean, somewhere else, and my dragging gait traverses silent

corridors, rooms furnished with the same playthings that my family has been accumulating since the times of the conquest, and rooms submerged in that false and hot darkness (of closed curtains) that invites one to take a nap or an even longer rest. I open the old wardrobe containing my used suits, the same closet which held the secrets of my great-grandparents. Consumed by time, not by use, I see that pair of shoes that I bought in Florence forty years ago. A woman I loved obliged me to buy them with the peremptory phrase that seems to be engraved almost intact in the sole: "I will not continue seeing you in those same butler's boots!" She took my hand and led me down the Via Tornabuoni, to the best shoe store in Florence, and with her index finger she selected this pair of brown shoes; with a gesture of her chin she indicated that they have me try them on. They pinched the tips of my toes (I couldn't speak) while she said "I like them, I like them, look how well they fit." They squeezed my instep while she said to the saleswoman "Yes, very good, they are perfect on him, he'll buy them." I could never wear them for more than twenty paces. Now I put them on again, and maybe I have shrunk a little with the years, for they almost fit.

Inert objects that awaken a memory sleeping among the ruins of time. Have I been a slave to memory, or have I been able to master a few corrections, mixing in invented fragments? There is the blue wool suit jacket, the one from the philosophy classes at the University. What's it still doing here, that decayed mummy? The professor explains the three powers of the soul: understanding, will and memory. Whence come the faculties of knowing, wanting and deciding. I have known; maybe and beyond maybe I have desired, but I cannot be sure that I have remembered everything. Despicable power, memory. It aspires to the impossible: to extend the past, to give a different duration to the lightning of existence. As though words could be enough to make the disappeared endure.

I am becoming paralyzed. The backward glance fleeces the future. Or the lack of a future leads us to look backwards. It is Lot's wife's syndrome, of which my friend Quitapesares speaks. This stone of bitterness remains, this salty statue. From which of the beams of this house will I hang? In which easy chair will I sit down to inhale the poison that I exhale? For I have resolved to die with the shoes on (those of the Via Tornabuoni, those that my Pietragrua made me buy), and raise my hand, once and for all, against everything that I am and everything that I have been.

The doors of the wardrobe are open, with my old shirts and suits consumed by time. Moth-eaten ties and the varied trends of fashion, the solid gold watch of my uncle the Archbishop (I wind it again and it still ticks, like my heart), the shiny cassock of Uncle Jacinto, my mother's wedding dress, her boxes of hats, the final letter from my father in Casablanca, "We are fine, we are talking and talking, we are having so much fun, take care." And it was them who should have been taking care of themselves. Them. I, without caring for myself, for years, I am now much older than my parents ever became. I. This owner of mine who is called me. I stand before this wardrobe, this mountain of memories. If I only had, like Job, someone to complain to. But chance, like the past, is deaf and indifferent to the curses of men.

I throw down my suits, I scatter them on the floor in

search of a memory that I don't recall. I have the feeling of having forgotten something fundamental. The point of the whole tangle, the source which could make sense of my whole existence. Nothing. One by one I review my memories. I have cultivated them, since they are so meager, day after day during these months of dictation; I have been sprucing them up, burnishing them, caressing them as a miser counts his treasure or a beggar chews his breadcrumbs. There, intact, is the suit in which I arrived in Italy, defeated, during the civil strife in my country. Blood, blood, blood. A nation drawn and quartered by idiotic and useless wars, by the abstract fanaticism of groups of lunatics. Minuscule guerrilla dictators, unscrupulous smugglers promoted to the heights of wealth, underhanded thieving politicians, vengeful and incapable generals, avaricious owners of cattle ranches and vacant lands without people.

They have obligated me to hate the place where I was born, and I have painstakingly cultivated this rancor. I would have preferred a rancor as short as a simple affront. It seems instead like a stale and rumpled verse: so brief the offense and so long the forgetting. Like those loves that maybe and beyond maybe I have had. Without that rancor and with those loves, my life would have been another, that which it should have been.

Ancient address books with stains of humidity. Names forgotten in geography and time, names which don't call up any faces. And photographs invaded by multicolored mildews where the faces glance, lacking names, from that yellowed black and white of years gone by. I will not open more boxes. I stuff into the shelves of the wardrobe all of these scraps of what I was. I don't surrender to the weakness of nostalgia, I refuse to repent. I close the door, I don't look back, I return to my desk to try to convince myself that what I have written is present. I reread these papers and I tell myself that I haven't remembered just to remember, to say or falsify that which was, but to construct myself, to know finally what I am as I fade from being. I have written to learn to be another. For the same reason I have read. This chattering prose will have grasped something of what my life wanted to be. I like believing that he who I am today, in the same circumstances as he who I was, would not repeat the actions of he who was called by my name. But life is not a rehearsal to learn to correct your mistakes. Only a book, that duplication of life, can serve as a rehearsal.

That one who I was, and who so loved life, would not be swallowing, one after the other, these sleeping pills. But that one who I was could not have had this full and unique perception of illness. Which is what invades me today. Everything that I have been ends up encircled, besieged by an evil which swells and torments me. Not a concrete, defined evil, but the certitude that death draws nigh. My illness is the will I have to die; I have become good friends with my approaching death.

I believe that if I anticipate the inevitable ending, this fight ends in a tie. I neither win nor lose. I end indulging in a right that all of us should have: that of dying as we want to. The end of this parenthesis; farewell and good luck to those who remain within. I am going to my delivery. Birth. When I write another period I will undress for the last time; I want to leave the world as I arrived in it, without even breathing.

I will imitate one of my Quitapesares', I will knot a plastic bag around my neck, I will lay down in my bed and I will embrace nothingness, I will again enter into it. Stop being. One ends up having, at the end, only one desire, to stop being. To not be. Be nothing more now. Not be. Soon I will be nothing. Be myself. To have been me, me, me. And to pass on to be nothing. Nothing, nothing, nothing

About the Author

HECTOR ABAD was born in Medellín, Colombia. He studied at a Catholic high school run by the Opus Dei. After pursuing several courses of study at Universidad Pontifica, he was expelled for writing an article critical of the Pope. He completed his degree in Modern Literature at the University of Turin. His father was assassinated in 1987, and Abad fled abroad for several years. He has published three books: *Malos Pensamientos* (1990), *Asuntos de un Hidalgo Disoluto* (1994), and *Tratado de Culinaria para Mujeres Tristes* (1996). He currently lives in Medellín, where he is the director of the magazine of the University of Antioquia and also manages a bookstore specializing in rare and antique books.